RETRIEVAL & RENEWAL

Ressourcement
IN CATHOLIC THOUGHT

The middle years of this century marked a particularly intense time of crisis and change in European society. During this period (1930-1950), a broad intellectual and spiritual movement arose within the European Catholic community, largely in response to the secularism that lay at the core of the crisis. The movement drew inspiration from earlier theologians and philosophers such as Möhler, Newman, Gardeil, Rousselot, and Blondel, as well as from men of letters like Charles Péguy and Paul Claudel.

The group of academic theologians included in the movement extended into Belgium and Germany, in the work of men like Emile Mersch, Dom Odo Casel, Romano Guardini, and Karl Adam. But above all the theological activity during this period centered in France. Led principally by the Jesuits at Fourviére and the Dominicans at Le Saulchoir, the French revival included many of the greatest names in twentieth-century Catholic thought: Henri de Lubac, Jean Daniélou, Yves Congar, Marie-Dominique Chenu, Louis Bouyer, and, in association, Hans Urs von Balthasar.

It is not true — as subsequent folklore has it — that those theologians represented any sort of self-conscious "school": indeed, the differences among them, for example, between Fourviére and Saulchoir, were important. At the same time, most of them were united in the double conviction that theology had to speak to the present situation, and that the condition for doing so faithfully lay in a recovery of the Church's past. In other words, they saw clearly that the first step in what later came to be known as *aggiornamento* had to be *ressourcement* — a rediscovery of the riches of the whole of the Church's two-thousand-year tradition. According to de Lubac, for example, all of his own works as well as the entire *Sources chrétiennes* collection are based on the presupposition that "the renewal of Christian vitality is linked at least partially to a renewed exploration of the periods and of the works where the Christian tradition is expressed with particular intensity."

In sum, for the *ressourcement* theologians theology involved a "return to the sources" of Christian faith, for the purpose of drawing out the meaning and significance of these sources for the critical questions of our time. What these theologians sought was a spiritual and intellectual communion with Christianity in its most vital moments as transmitted to us in its classic texts, a communion which would nourish, invigorate, and rejuvenate twentieth-century Catholicism.

The *ressourcement* movement bore great fruit in the documents of the Second Vatican Council and has deeply influenced the work of Pope John Paul II and Cardinal Joseph Ratzinger, Prefect of the Sacred Congregation of the Doctrine of the Faith.

The present series is rooted in this twentieth-century renewal of theology, above all as the renewal is carried in the spirit of de Lubac and von Balthasar. In keeping with that spirit, the series understands *ressourcement* as revitalization: a return to the sources, for the purpose of developing a theology that will truly meet the challenges of our time. Some of the features of the series, then, will be:

- a return to classical (patristic-mediaeval) sources;
- a renewed interpretation of St. Thomas;
- a dialogue with the major movements and thinkers of the twentieth century, with particular attention to problems associated with the Enlightenment, modernity, liberalism.

The series will publish out-of-print or as yet untranslated studies by earlier authors associated with the *ressourcement* movement. The series also plans to publish works by contemporary authors sharing in the aim and spirit of this earlier movement. This will include interpretations of de Lubac and von Balthasar and, more generally, any works in theology, philosophy, history, literature, and the arts which give renewed expression to an authentic Catholic sensibility.

The editor of the Ressourcement series, David L. Schindler, is Gagnon Professor of Fundamental Theology at the John Paul II Institute in Washington, D.C., and editor of the North American edition of *Communio: International Catholic Review,* a federation of journals in thirteen countries founded in Europe in 1972 by Hans Urs von Balthasar, Jean Daniélou, Henri de Lubac, Joseph Ratzinger, and others.

RETRIEVAL & RENEWAL

Ressourcement

IN CATHOLIC THOUGHT

available

Mysterium Paschale
by Hans Urs von Balthasar

The Letter on Apologetics *and* History and Dogma
by Maurice Blondel

Letters from Lake Como:
Explorations in Technology and the Human Race
by Romano Guardini

The Portal of the Mystery of Hope
Charles Péguy

In the Beginning:
A Catholic Understanding of the Story of Creation and the Fall
by Cardinal Joseph Ratzinger

Hans Urs von Balthasar: A Theological Style
by Angelo Scola

forthcoming

Prayer: The Mission of the Church
Jean Daniélou

The Discovery of God
Henri de Lubac

The Portal
of the Mystery
# of Hope

Charles Péguy

Translated by

David Louis Schindler, Jr.

WILLIAM B. EERDMANS PUBLISHING COMPANY
GRAND RAPIDS, MICHIGAN

Originally published as *Le porche du mystère de la deuxième vertu*
© 1929 Gallimard, Paris
Critical edition, with preface and notes by Jean Bastaire,
© 1986 by Gallimard, Paris

English translation of the 1986 critical edition
© 1996 Wm. B. Eerdmans Publishing Co.
2140 Oak Industrial Drive N.E., Grand Rapids, Michigan 49505

Printed in the United States of America

01 00 99 98 97 96   7 6 5 4 3 2 1

Library of Congress Cataloging-in-Publication Data

Péguy, Charles, 1873-1914
    [Porche du mystère de la deuxième vertu. English]
    The portal of the mystery of hope / Charles Péguy; translated by
David Louis Schindler, Jr.
        p.   cm. — (Ressourcement)
    Includes bibliographical references
    ISBN 978-0-8028-0899-8 (pbk.: alk. paper)
    I. Schindler, David Louis, Jr., 1970-   . II. Title. III. Series:
Ressourcement (Grand Rapids, Mich.)
PQ2631.E25P6513   1996
841'.912 — dc 20   96-3471
                                                          CIP

CONTENTS

PREFACE

A great text not only is beautiful; it creates life, it has a seminal influence. Such is *Les Misérables* or Rimbaud's *Illuminations*. Among Péguy's writings, none has fulfilled this germinal role as much as *The Portal of the Mystery of Hope*. Countless readers have benefited from it. Many have drawn from it the strength of an inward resurrection.

The scope of the *Portal* lies far beyond the horizons of a particular generation. Its point of impact is the wound in each person's heart that leaks out his soul's blood. In response to this anemia of being, where one no longer desires anything but sleep and death, Péguy proposes a radical cure. He does not do this by means of rational arguments, nor even less by admonitions or injunctions. Péguy loathes morality and he ridicules psychology. His is a spiritual therapy. Its instrument is the poem.

There is no authentic poet who is not also an adventurer of the spirit. Péguy exemplifies this definition, which excludes all hedonists of the pen and miasmic crooners. One does not come under his *Portal*, with its simple allure, without risking everything. Or rather, one is pushed there by the supreme threat of losing heart and falling into the void.

Péguy himself undertook the writing of this poem in the midst of anguish, among the fields of ruin. Apart from his children, there was nothing left to give meaning to his life. The betrayal of the Dreyfus Affair and the corruption of socialism had sapped his revolutionary spirit, poisoned the management of his *Cahiers,* and undermined his home. And, to culminate his disgrace, Péguy was consumed by an impossible love.

Thus, the *Portal,* this hymn to hope, sprang forth from the most profound despair. It is not coincidental that such a candid series of pages closes with the night of Good Friday and the burial of Jesus. It ends, however, not in agony, but in the soothing of a mysterious rest, which leaves us as yet uncertain if it will emerge into Easter, even though this is suggested. It is as if the artist's exhaustion, after his invisible wrestling with the angel, finally reveals itself in his pained signature at the base of the painting.

The work's existential tension, which allows it to avoid more than a few traps, undoubtedly owes itself to these circumstances. The poem has too often been disserved by an inane reading in selected bits, evacuating the tenderness of the work of its purified suffering and transformed bitterness. In reality, the *Portal* is a literal incarnation of what the text says of the bad water become a living fountain. Carried by hope, poetry here fulfills its highest office: not embellishment, but conversion, resurrection from death, and a drawing from misery into the light.

At the same time, it rediscovers a theological and mystical function that occidental Christianity had neglected in its poetry for many centuries, abandoning to doubtful and more or less heretical visionaries what orthodox thinkers had let slip from their dialectical speculations: the flesh of the religious experience, the breath of contact with the ontological.

Theological poetry renews a relationship with the great symbolical tradition, which had thrived up until the twelfth century, and which oriental Christianity has maintained even to the present day. This is not to say that it thinks by means of myths, those vast mother-images that are an intensification of a fundamental experience. Instead, it thinks by means of symbols. And rather than being borrowed from the abstract universals of concepts, these symbols are drawn from concrete, phenomenological, and historical reality. Myth itself is nothing other than a symbol, albeit a privileged one.

The theological poet, like the symbolic theologian, proceeds from a reading of Creation. For him, the world is another sacred Scripture, in which he finds recounted a sublime event. It is the same event as that recounted in the other Book, which the patriarchs, the prophets, and the evangelists have put into words. There are thus two pathways to Revelation. Far from being redundant, these two ways echo each other. It is as if, from the beginning, the divine Word, while taking form in the sacred texts, had also wished to become incarnate in a cosmic flesh.

When Péguy evokes the soul-horse and the body-plow, when he contemplates the rain of bad days that are soaked up by the good soil of souls, when he passes hope on as one would pass on holy water at a funeral, he does not do so like some creator of pleasant images, as effective as they are lucid. No, he is much more than that: he is a faithful reader who unveils the divine reality from within the human reality. With his crafty tone and his *gros sabots,* he comprehends the language of God. It should not surprise us, then, that he makes God speak.

For, far from being merely a literary technique, this audacity is consistent with an inner logic. None but God could pronounce the essential word that, before it became incarnate personally in Jesus, he had inscribed in each creature. If he handles the language of beings and of things with a sovereign ease, it is because he is their author. And if Péguy is their miraculous scribe, it is because he effaces himself before the Father of the Word. Péguy remarks simply, "God says." Or as the prophets had affirmed, "The Word of Yahweh." In either case, God proclaims himself in proclaiming the world.

This thus explains one of the most disconcerting aspects of the *Portal:* the down-to-earth, almost banal, side of this vision. The seemingly insignificant image he chooses suddenly glows with a hidden meaning. And it is not destroyed, but rather magnified by this unfolding of meaning. All of a sudden, the mute speak; the silence of the humdrum days comes undone. An unusual song of praise rises from this unremarkable universe, from which we had expected nothing but the ordinary.

The poem also weds a stream of familiar and familial images — children, father, mother, uncle — to a mass of biblical and liturgical quotations: from Matthew, Luke, John, the *Hail Mary,* and the *Salve Regina,* not to mention the poets Villon, La Fontaine, and Hugo. "Everything serves to make a meal," as popular wisdom would have it, and Péguy himself would concur. All things are open to the investigation of love and to spiritual elucidation.

What is admirable in the *Portal* is that with earthly words, with carnal images that have nothing of philosophy in them, with the movements of the heart that are those of any creature, Péguy revolutionizes Christianity in the sense that, as he says elsewhere, "a revolution is a call from a less perfect tradition to a more perfect tradition." His theology of hope definitively undermines Jansenism and prepares the majestic way of the Gospel, which has too long been encumbered by the fears that mock the cross of Christ.

Not only does the author of the *Portal* reverse his personal drama of failure and exile, converting distress into tenderness and dereliction into creative abandon, but he similarly inverts a more general ontological drama, which has haunted him since his youth and which is the heart of his meditation on the figure of Joan of Arc: the failure and exile of the damned. In a staggering intuition, he makes damnation into God's own failure and exile.

To avoid this, God is reduced to hoping in the sinner, just as the sinner hopes in God. God makes the first move. Here, as in love and in all things, God takes the initiative, he sets the example. Moreover, doesn't this represent the most perfect love, wherein the lover puts himself in a state of dependence on the beloved, relies on the beloved? God relies on the sinner, and fears for him in the hope that the sinner will mend his ways and, like the prodigal son, collapse into God's arms.

Péguy's anthropology is no less fecund. He manages to avoid all the temptations of Manichaeanism and makes the human being a whole in which the body and the soul "sym-bolize" (are in union with) rather than "dia-bolize" (are divided against) each other. In a striking image, echoed in the similarly beautiful images of his poem *Eve*, Péguy compares the body and the soul to two hands joined in prayer or two wrists bound in sin. Together, they undergo the same adventure. And the poet also has the audacity to overturn the proposition that is, alas, far too common, though it is not Christian. This belief suggests that the angels are fortunate not to be burdened with a body. For Péguy, however, this is an imperfection because, lacking the "very body of Jesus," the angels are unable to imitate him.

The central mystery of Christianity is the Incarnation. According to the traditional adage of the Fathers of the Church, God truly became man so that we could truly become God. All mistrust of the flesh, all hatred of the temporal, is therefore an abomination, for it is a mistrust and hatred of the very real conditions that the Word has assumed in order to redeem them. God so loved the world — and not only souls, but bodies, the earth, creation — that he sent his only Son.

One creature is the prototype of the new humanity redeemed by Christ: Mary, the mother of Jesus. She is superior both to humans and to angels, because while she is carnal like humans, she is also pure like the angels, without the shadow of sin. She alone is a perfect imitation of Jesus, because she alone is wholly terrestrial and wholly divinized. Péguy's worship of Mary, far from being an overly devout pietism, is an exultation of the temporal by the eternal, and a glorification of the flesh by the spirit.

Likewise, the place the author of the *Portal* gives to childhood is at odds with all childishness. It takes an adult to be immature. Children are new and full of energy. With the freshness of the renewed earth, their innocence is explosive. They know no doubt. In the gratuity of their being, they run for the sake of running, and not for the sake of arriving somewhere. They are pure *élan*. That is why they are irresistible.

Between her two sisters Faith and Love, Hope is a little girl who guides all things. Péguy's happy image is so fitting that she has circled the entire world. The whole of the *Portal* resumes itself in her because, as it is expressed by the "puer eternus" (eternal child) of the collective unconscious, there exists a connection between childhood and resurrection, and Hope brings the grace that we anticipate from Easter.

JEAN BASTAIRE

NOTE

The Portal of the Mystery of Hope is an independent work, capable of standing on its own. It also forms the second panel of a triptych, which Péguy had dreamed of making into a polyptych. As he explained to Joseph Lotte on April 1, 1910, "I envision a dozen volumes" (*Lettres et entretiens,* collected by Marcel Péguy, éd. de Paris, 1954, p. 68). Only three are completed. *The Mystery of the Charity of Joan of Arc,* published January 16, 1910, is a considerably augmented reprise of the beginning of his first *Joan of Arc,* a vast work of drama written thirteen years earlier. *The Portal of the Mystery of Hope,* which came out October 22, 1911, continues this work in the form of an immense monologue. *The Mystery of the Holy Innocents,* appearing March 24, 1912, carries on the soliloquy, occasionally returning to a dialogue form akin to that of the *Mystery of the Charity.*

This series shows a strange and irresistible evolution toward interiority. The first *Joan of Arc* was a dramatic work of Shakespearian dimensions, with multiple characters and several scene changes. The *Mystery of the Charity* is an oratorio, with three characters and a single setting. The *Portal* and the *Holy Innocents* are a meditative speech by a single character, having no other setting but one's own heart. We have thus moved from an epic drama to a theological poem.

Péguy began the writing of the *Portal* on July 9, 1910, as he explained in a conversation with his friend Lotte (*Lettres et entretiens,* pp. 77-78). He interrupted his project almost immediately in August and September in order to write an important prose work, *Victor-Marie, comte Hugo.* On September 17, referring to the *Portal,* he told Lotte that his "second Joan of Arc would appear on the Feast of the Epiphany," at the start of the following year (*Lettres et entretiens,* p. 79). In short, the substance of the work seems to have been written between January and August, 1911.

On March 17, 1910, the day after the publication of the *Mystery of the Charity,* Jacques Copeau requested a fragment of the work in progress for *La Nouvelle Revue française,* a young periodical that had just entered its second year (*Feuillets de l'Amitié Charles Péguy* no. 5, January–March

1979, p. 4). Péguy did not say no, and even made a promise to Gide. During the elaboration of the *Portal,* Jean Schlumberger returned to the author several times with the same request. Finally, Péguy decided that he would prefer to print the poem in its entirety without any prepublication (*Correspondance Péguy-Schlumberger, L'Amitié Charles Péguy,* no. 5, January–March 1979, pp. 55-56). *La Nouvelle Revue française* restricted itself to printing an excerpt, December 1, 1911, under the section heading "Readings."

Appearing October 22, 1911, in the fourth *cahier* of the thirteenth series, the *Portal* almost immediately enjoyed a second printing with the publisher Emile-Paul. This editor continued to distribute the work until the poet's death in 1914. All of Péguy's works, revised or unrevised, then passed over to the Editions de la Nouvelle Revue française, edited by Gaston Gallimard, who assured himself of their exclusive rights. The *Portal* was reprinted in 1918 as volume five of the *Oeuvres complètes,* along with the *Mystery of the Charity,* and followed in 1929 by a standard edition in the white collection, which has since been continuously reprinted. In 1941, it was printed as part of the Pléiade edition of the *Oeuvres poétiques complètes,* under the direction of Marcel Péguy. A new Pléiade edition appeared in 1957, enriched by notes and variations added by Marcel Péguy. The 1975 edition only reprinted these same notes with the text. A critical edition of the *Portal* does not exist.

When it was first issued, the *Portal* did not receive the same enthusiastic response that met the *Mystery of the Charity.* Several factors contribute to this silence (which, five months later, became a "leaden silence" for the *Holy Innocents*). On the one hand, it is normal that the sequel to a work would not make the same impact in the press, nor win the same favor with the public, as would the first text. Interest created by curiosity dulls quickly. On the other hand, the success of the *Mystery of the Charity* was due in large part to a political exploit based upon a misunderstanding (the repentance of a former Dreyfus advocate), which Péguy hastened to clear up in two vigorous essays, *Notre jeunesse* and *Victor-Marie, comte Hugo.* Finally, with the failure to obtain the Grand Prize from the Académie française and with the polemic aimed at Fernand Laudet, the director of the *Revue hebdomadaire,* the year 1911 saw Péguy throwing himself into new battles. Though they periodically succeeded in reviving interest in him, these battles ultimately ended by banishing him irretrievably to the margins. During his last three months of life, Péguy was an author who was not so much ignored as mistrusted, as much on the right as on the left, and about whom people kept their silence.

For all of that, certain private testimonies were all the more sweet to the heart of the poet. Here, we present those by Gide, Schlumberger, Bremond, and Rolland. Along with these, we add a more recent appreciation, written in 1962 by the Catholic theologian Hans Urs von Balthasar, who expresses with a sufficient amplitude the greatness of the *Portal of the Mystery of Hope.*

APPRECIATIONS

My dear Péguy, you are decidedly a prodigious gentleman. This *Portal of the Mystery of Hope* astonishes me perhaps even more than *The Mystery of the Charity of Joan of Arc.* I read it yesterday all in one sitting, as one ought to read you, setting aside all other activity. I felt that I was at the organ, playing one of Bach's fugues. . . .

> *André Gide*
>
> (Letter to Péguy, October 27, 1911, in the *Bulletin des amis d'André Gide,* no. 62 [April 1984]: 190)

I cannot hold myself back, my dear Péguy, from expressing to you my emotion. It was not easy to disappoint us. The first *Joan of Arc* (i.e. *The Mystery of the Charity*) was raised to such a level of pathos that we were all ready to find this one less beautiful. You seem to leave us in a state of unsatisfied waiting because you show us Joan of Arc only by allusion. But in the friendly company of the men and women saints who adorn this portal, we wait quite willingly. You delight in a religious spirit that is daring and yet constrained; sensible and yet, as you would say, adventurous. And, above all, you delight in a poetry that is so new, a poetry that is so generous, so disdainful of the rest of our little ceremonies. And we think of you each time our children present their heads to us for a kiss.

> *Jean Schlumberger*
>
> (Letter to Péguy, October 24, 1911, in *L'Amitié Charles Péguy,* no. 6 [January–March]: 56-57)

Dear Sir, it is absolutely beautiful. Your fresh and new little hope, who speaks as they will still be speaking in three hundred years — and forever — has all the living grace, flesh, and blood of the Trojan statues. I have been thinking of this poor Huysmans with his pretense of *primitivism*. I enjoyed him because he was sincere and because the pharisees detested him, but what a difference, what differences! He is a misogynist, while your little hope is a woman; he cannot even look at a child without grinding his teeth and your hope is a tiny little girl. . . .

Finally, I am delighted and what is better, very deeply touched, and better still, grateful — not only for myself, the insignificant person that I am and who ought to have discovered all of this in the *law* and the *prophets*, and in Villon as well, but for the masses whom no one evangelizes anymore and to whom you have brought the good news.

Henri Bremond

(Letter to Péguy, November 7, 1911, in *Feuillets de L'Amitié Charles Péguy*, no. 171 [September 10, 1975]: 10-11)

I have read the second *cahier* of Péguy's *Joan of Arc* — this title that comes straight from the Middle Ages: *The Portal of the Mystery of Hope*. . . . With all of its monstrous and exasperating faults, it is a work of genius. I am no longer capable of reading anything after Péguy. All the rest is just literature. His is the most genial force in European literature. What is more, it is purely and strictly French.

Romain Rolland

(*Journal*, beginning 1912, quoted by Alfred Saffrey in *Une amitié française, correspondance Péguy* — *R. Rolland* [Albin Michel, 1955], 154-55)

Péguy, who was certainly not a theologian given to compartmentalising, had brought his insights, once achieved, to completion in a breakthrough into a comprehensive theology of hope — by means of patient contemplation of the one reality that is at once natural and supernatural, by an unceasing process of *approfondissement* and assimilation. And this theology of hope makes its presence felt today, gently but irresistibly, by a structural shift in the whole theological edifice. . . .

So the whole of Péguy's art and theology flow more and more towards prayer without one ever being able to say precisely whether this prayer is a dialogue or a monologue on God's part. It is a dialogue with God (predominantly so in *Jeanne*), but one which is constantly developing into a monologue of God the Father, addressed without distinction to his Son, to the men he has created and to himself. It is a form of "theology as Trinitarian conversation," never realised prior to Péguy, which could only be risked by a poet using a simple and popular style of utterance that avoids any show of sublimity and yet does not for a moment degenerate into "mateyness" and false familiarity. Only faith in the Holy Spirit can allow God to speak in such a way.

Hans Urs von Balthasar

(*The Glory of the Lord,* vol. 3: *Studies in Theological Style: Lay Styles,* tr. Andrew Louth, John Saward, Martin Simon and Rowan Williams, ed. Joseph Fessio, S.J., and John Riches [San Francisco: Ignatius Press, 1986], 494, 506.)

TRANSLATOR'S PREFACE

Because the reader may find Péguy's unconventional and occasionally awkward style somewhat of an obstacle at the outset, we preface his poem with a few brief comments. Here, as in all great works of art, the form bears an intrinsic relation to the content; to reach the heart of the poet's ideas, therefore, we are obliged to consider them in their incarnated form, within the context of the whole of the work.

In approaching Péguy, it is perhaps particularly important to avoid separating ideas from their concrete expression, for he himself had filled many pages in his *Cahiers* with passionate discussions of the dangers of "any arbitrary separation" of the abstract and the concrete, the spiritual and the "carnal." Indeed, his shift to poetry as a vehicle for communication (which occurred relatively late in his life as an author), may be seen as the fruit of much thinking on this subject. As Alexander Dru argues in his study on Péguy, the best approach to the whole of Péguy's work begins with his poetry. He is not a thinker who also happened to write poetry; rather, his poetry itself is the expression of what all of his writing sought to attain.

Why is this so? The key, according to Dru, is the imagination, for it is here that the primordial inspiration is received in its wholeness, before its differentiation into image and idea, form and content. Péguy elucidates this notion at length in his pseudonymous *Commentary* on his poem *Eve*. In this commentary, Péguy explores the relationship between the image and the idea, insisting that it would be wrong to think that the image "comes after" the idea, as if it were just one possible form among many of expressing the content of the idea. If this were the case, the reader would be able to understand the poet only when he was finally able to extract the idea from the image, leaving the image behind as an unfortunate, but necessary, mediation of the poet's thought. This, however, is precisely what Péguy wished to reject. For him, the idea and the image are born together in the same moment within the imagination. The "freedom" of this initial inspiration is then manifested in the "order" of the poem, as the poet works to give birth to what he has conceived. The unity of the image and the idea as it exists in the pristine imagination is thus preserved in the poem, with the "abstract immediately nourished by the concrete, and the concrete illuminated continually by the abstract." Péguy thus opposes, on the one hand, the rationalists who would subordinate the image to the idea: theirs is a sterile order without freedom. On the other hand, he opposes the irrationalists who would subordinate the idea to the image: theirs is a confused freedom without order.

It is perhaps not coincidental that Péguy begins to write poetry at roughly the same time as his return to Catholicism. His poetry, of course, is generally about the Christian life, but there is a deeper relation between the two than just this. The mysteries of the Incarnation and the Blessed Virgin, which stand at the heart of Péguy's faith, embody the same themes contained in his discussion of poetry: in both mysteries, we find the intersection of the realms of the spiritual and the carnal, the abstract and the concrete, the eternal and the temporal. Christianity is not an abstract philosophical or theological system that subsequently expresses itself in the Gospel "images" and eventually in the structure of the Church, any more than the poem is just a convenient expression of the writer's ideas. Indeed, the unity of the whole of the Catholic faith, including the visible form of the Church, is contained within, and inseparable from, the concrete person of Jesus Christ and the concrete person of Mary. As Péguy says in the *Portal,* Jesus' "words" were pronounced carnally in time. We, as Christians, are not just the hearers of the word; we are to give flesh to his words just as Mary gave her flesh to the infant in her womb. In this sense, we become a continuation of the Incarnation: "He depends on us to grant his eternal words, pronounced carnally in time, a second eternity, an eternity of flesh and blood." Were we to fail, his words would "collapse fleshless."

The work of the Incarnation will not be complete, says Péguy, until the whole of creation is assumed — all of time, all of the finite, all of the carnal, up to the least of the sinners, must be taken up into God's life. God wishes to be glorified in every aspect of creation, but he is best glorified in the virtue of hope, for it is in hope that a person expresses most profoundly the greatest trust in God, the greatest confidence in God's love. The child therefore becomes a central image of the *Portal,* because the child, in absolute helplessness and dependence on parents, is one who "smiles inwardly" with the complete assurance of being safely borne along by the parents' love. To hope means thus to recognize the boundless grace of God as the reality that surrounds and supports us, the reality in which we bathe and remake our being, the reality that "accompanies us into our greatest follies" and "into the shamefulness of our sin," unceasingly reminding us that God's love for us remains constant despite our own inconstancy. Every creature who comes to hope in God thus represents God's own triumph, and causes God to say, marveling at his own glory, "My grace must, indeed, be great."

According to Péguy, God, too, is joined with his creatures in hoping: He has entered into creation out of love, and asks his creature to respond in love, and this means in freedom. Since freedom is essential to love, God cannot force himself on the one he loves. Instead, he himself is forced to await the freedom of his creature, forced to "hope for the sinner." But, nevertheless, God does not stand apart, waiting passively for this freedom. He has gone out to meet his creature, he has truly "taken the initiative" — indeed, as Péguy says elsewhere, God has "sacrificed everything to obtain this freedom." This "sacrifice" that God makes in his supreme hope for the sinner once again reveals the glory of his love, and it does so by way of a paradox, for it is precisely the omnipotence of God's love that allows him to risk the humiliation and powerlessness of the Crucifixion.

Péguy's vision of hope manifests itself in the peculiarity of his poetic style. As another French writer, Romain Rolland, has said of Péguy, "I know of no other writer who has ever made God speak in such a manner." It is undoubtedly the colloquial character of Péguy's idiom that first strikes us as unusual. In the *Portal,* God speaks to us as a merciful, as a hopeful, Father, who tries to elicit hope from his creatures. His language is filled with images drawn from the basic experiences of life, rather than sophisticated argumentation aimed at an elite few. There is not a trace of condescension in his tone: God does not speak from the sublime heights of heaven, looking down at the world from an infinite distance. Rather, having assumed everything human, he speaks from within the world; he speaks, as it were, as "one of us." Like an old French peasant, he is absolutely serious about what he is saying, and yet an affectionate humor pervades every sentence. His manner is gentle and compassionate, and yet always firm. But what is perhaps most remarkable in Péguy's style is that the familiar tone of God's speech never compromises God's infinite greatness. We never once forget that God is the Creator, and if he does not speak from infinitely above us, it is only because he himself has crossed the distance out of his gratuitous love. What Péguy says in the poem of the Blessed Virgin can therefore also be said, inversely, of God: He makes himself infinitely lowly precisely because he is infinitely lofty. And so, Péguy's profound insight into the nature of God's love is carried all the way through into the style of speech that communicates it.

Finally, Péguy's insistence on the incarnational nature of God's love reveals itself in the fact that God speaks, in the *Portal*, through a concrete character in a drama. The *Portal* is not just a long free-verse poem uttered from "out of the blue"; rather, as the title suggests, it is in fact a play. The "portal" refers to the entranceway of medieval cathedrals, whose tympana often depicted a Christian mystery. The cathedral's portal was also where Christian mystery plays were typically enacted. If we keep in mind that the *Portal* is a play, we are better able to appreciate the conversational quality of the writing. Madame Gervaise, God's "mouthpiece" in the poem, addresses her monologue to the young Joan of Arc, who remains silent throughout. She speaks in short phrases, pausing after each one as if to make sure that "Jeannette" has understood it. And, as in any conversation, Madame Gervaise often digresses from a thought, only to pick it up again several lines — or even pages! — later. These long pauses, along with the constant repetition of a word or phrase, create a slow, meditative rhythm. The rhythm, however, never becomes heavy, because each repetition adds a new dimension, and so deepens the meditation at every turn.

Thus, all of the elements of Péguy's work — his concrete images, his colloquial idiom, his striking insights into the heart of God — gather together into a single, powerful statement of the central place of hope in the Christian life. And it is unlikely that anyone who has heard this "word of hope" will ever again be able to silence it in his or her heart.

DAVID LOUIS SCHINDLER, JR.

NON SOLVM IN MEMORIAM
SED IN INTENTIONEM

Not only in memory of
but dedicated to

our friend and our brother Eddy Marix

Etville sur le Rhin, 2 August 1880
Etville sur le Rhin, 31 August 1908

notably in memory of
the cahier he made

for Palm Sunday and
Easter Sunday of the
year 1905.[1]

a cahier for All Saints day
and for All Souls day, from the thirteenth series;

second cahier in preparation
for the five-hundredth anniversary
of the birth of Joan of Arc,
which will come on the Feast of the Epiphany
in the year 1912

THE PORTAL
OF THE MYSTERY
OF HOPE

MADAME GERVAISE² *reenters*

MADAME GERVAISE

The faith that I love the best, says God, is hope.

Faith doesn't surprise me.
It's not surprising.
I am so resplendent in my creation.
In the sun and the moon and in the stars.
In all of my creatures.
In the stars of the firmament and in the fish of the sea.
In the universe of my creatures.
Upon the face of the earth and upon the face of the waters.
In the movements of the stars in heaven.
In the wind that blows upon the sea and in the wind that blows in the
        valley.
In the peaceful valley.
In the hushed and hidden valley.
In the plants and in the beasts and in the beasts of the forest.
And in man.
My creature.
In peoples and in men and in kings and in peoples.
In man and in woman his companion.
And especially in children.
My creatures.
In the gaze and in the voice of children.
Because children are more my creatures.
    Than men are.
They haven't yet been defeated by life.
    On earth.
And of them all they are my servants.

Above all.

And the voice of children is purer than the voice of the wind in the
calm of the valley.

In the hushed and hidden valley.

And the gaze of children is purer than the blue of the sky, than the
milky sky, and than a star's rays in the peaceful night.

Yes, I am so resplendent in my creation.

Upon the face of the mountains and on the face of the plains.

In bread and in wine and in the man who tills and in the man who
sows and in the harvest of grain and in the harvest of grapes.

In the light and in the darkness.

And in the heart of man, which is what is most profound in the world.

The created world.

So profound it is impenetrable to all eyes.

Except my own.

In the tempest that rocks the waves and in the tempest that shakes the
leaves.

The leaves of the trees in the forest.

And conversely in the calm of a beautiful evening.

In the sands of the sea and in the stars that are grains of sand in the
sky.

In the stone of the threshold and in the stone of the hearth and in the
stone of the altar.

In prayer and in sacraments.

In men's houses and in the church that is my house on earth.

In my creature the eagle who flies upon the peaks.

The kingly eagle who has a wingspan of at least two meters and
sometimes three.[3]

And in my creature the ant who creeps and who hoards pettily.

In the ground.

In the ant, my servant.

And even in the serpent.

In my servant the ant, my tiny servant, who hoards greedily like a
miser.

Who works like one unhappy and who has no break and who has no
rest.

But death and but the long sleep of winter.

I am so resplendent in all of my creation.
In the tiny one, in my tiny creature, in my tiny servant, in the tiny ant.
Who hoards greedily, like man.
Like tiny man.
And who digs tunnels in the dirt.
In the cellars of the earth.
For stingily gathering his treasures.
His worldly treasures.
Pitifully.
And even in the serpent.
Who tricked the woman and who for that crawls on his belly.
And who is my creature and who is my servant.
The serpent who tricked the woman.
My servant.
Who tricked man my servant.
I am so resplendent in my creation.
In all that happens to men and to peoples, and to the poor.
And even to the rich.
Who don't want to be my creatures.
And who take refuge.
From being my servants.
In all the good and evil that man has done and undone.
(And I am above it all, because I am the master, and I do what he has
        undone and I undo what he has done.)
And unto the temptation to sin.
Even.
And in all that happened to my son.
Because of man.
My creature.
Whom I had created.
In the conception, in the birth and in the life and in the death of my
        son.
And in the holy sacrifice of the Mass.

In every birth and in every life.

And in every death.
And in eternal life that will never end.
That will overcome all death.

I am so resplendent in my creation.

That in order really not to see me these poor people would have to be
blind.

Charity, says God, that doesn't surprise me.
It's not surprising.
These poor creatures are so miserable that unless they had a heart of
stone, how could they not have love for each other.
How could they not love their brothers.
How could they not take the bread from their own mouth, their daily
bread, in order to give it to the unhappy children who pass by.
And my son had such a love for them.

My son their brother.
Such a great love.

But hope, says God, that is something that surprises me.
Even me.
That is surprising.

That these poor children see how things are going and believe that
tomorrow things will go better.
That they see how things are going today and believe that they will go
better tomorrow morning.
That is surprising and it's by far the greatest marvel of our grace.
And I'm surprised by it myself.
And my grace must indeed be an incredible force.
And must flow freely and like an inexhaustible river.
Since the first time it flowed and since it has forever been flowing.
In my natural and supernatural creation.
In my spiritual and carnal and yet spiritual creation.
In my eternal and temporal and yet eternal creation.
Mortal and immortal.

And that time, oh that time, since that time that it flowed like a river
of blood, from the pierced side of my son.
What must my grace, and the strength of my grace, be so that this
little hope, vacillating at the breath of sin, trembling with
every wind, anxious at the slightest breath,
be as constant, remain as faithful, as righteous, as pure; and invincible,
and immortal, and impossible to extinguish; as that little flame
in the sanctuary.
That burns eternally in the faithful lamp.
One trembling flame has endured the weight of worlds.
One vacillating flame has endured the weight of time.
One anxious flame has endured the weight of nights.
Since the first time my grace flowed for the creation of the world.
Since my grace has been flowing forever for the preservation of the
world.
Since the time that the blood of my son flowed for the salvation of the
world.

A flame impossible to reach, impossible to extinguish with the breath
of death.

What surprises me, says God, is hope.
And I can't get over it.
This little hope who seems like nothing at all.
This little girl hope.[4]
Immortal.

Because my three virtues, says God.
The three virtues, my creatures.
My daughters, my children.
Are themselves like my other creatures.
Of the race of men.
Faith is a loyal Wife.
Charity is a Mother.
An ardent mother, noble-hearted.
Or an older sister who is like a mother.
Hope is a little girl, nothing at all.
Who came into the world on Christmas day just this past year.

Who is still playing with her snowman.
With her German fir trees painted with frost.
And with her ox and her ass made of German wood. Painted.
And with her manger stuffed with straw that the animals don't eat.
Because they're made of wood.
And yet it's this little girl who will endure worlds.
This little girl, nothing at all.
She alone, carrying the others, who will cross worlds past.

As the star guided the three kings from the deepest Orient.
Toward the cradle of my son.
Like a trembling flame.
She alone will guide the Virtues and Worlds.

One flame will pierce the eternal shadows.

The priest says.
Minister of God, the priest says:

What are the three theological virtues?

The child responds:

The three theological virtues are Faith, Hope, and Charity.

— *Why are Faith, Hope, and Charity called theological virtues?*

— *Faith, Hope, and Charity are called theological virtues because they
    relate immediately to God.*

— *What is Hope?*

— *Hope is the supernatural virtue by which we await God with
    confidence, his grace in this world and eternal glory in the next.*

— *Make an act of Hope.*

— *My God, I hope, with a firm confidence, that you will give me, by the*

merits of Jesus Christ, your grace in this world, and, if I observe
your commandments, your glory in the next, because you have
promised it to me, and because you are supremely faithful in your
promises.[5]

We too often forget, my child,[6] that hope is a virtue, that it is a
theological virtue, and that of all the virtues, and of the three
theological virtues, it is perhaps the most pleasing to God.
That it is assuredly the most difficult, that it is perhaps the only
difficult one, and that it is undoubtedly the most pleasing to
God.

Faith is obvious. Faith can walk on its own. To believe you just have to
let yourself go, you just need to look around. In order not to
believe, you would have to do violence to yourself, frustrate
yourself. Harden yourself. Run yourself backwards, turn
yourself inside-out, thwart yourself. Faith is completely natural,
easy-going, simple, easy-coming. Very easy-coming. Very
easy-going. It's a woman that everyone knows, a nice old lady,
a nice old parishioner, a nice woman from the parish, an old
grandmother. She tells stories about the old days, what
happened in the old days.

In order not to believe, my child, you would have to shut your eyes
and plug your ears. In order not to see, not to believe.

Unfortunately Charity is obvious. Charity can walk on its own. To love
your neighbor you just have to let yourself go, you just have to
look around at all the distress. In order not to love you would
have to do violence to yourself, torture yourself, torment
yourself, frustrate yourself. Harden yourself. Hurt yourself.
Distort yourself. Run yourself backwards, turn yourself
inside-out. Thwart yourself. Charity is completely natural,
simple, overflowing, very easy-coming. It's the first movement
of the heart. And the first movement is the right one. Charity
is a mother and a sister.

In order not to love your neighbor, my child, you would have to shut
     your eyes and plug your ears.
To so many cries of distress.

But hope is not obvious. Hope does not come on its own.
To hope, my child, you would have to be quite fortunate, to have
     obtained, received a great grace.

It's faith that is easy and not believing that would be impossible. It's
     charity that is easy and not loving that would be impossible.
     But it's hoping that is difficult.

ashamedly and in a low voice.

And the easy thing and the tendency is to despair and that's the great
     temptation.

The little hope moves forward in between her two older sisters and one
     scarcely notices her.
On the path to salvation, on the earthly path, on the rocky path of
     salvation, on the interminable road, on the road in between
     her two older sisters the little hope
Pushes on.
In between her two older sisters.
The one who's married.
And the one who's a mother.
And no one pays attention, the Christian people don't pay attention,
     except to the two older sisters.
The first and the last.
Who attend to the most pressing things first.
Who attend to the moment at hand.
To each passing moment.
The Christian people only see the two older sisters, don't notice
     anything but the two older sisters.
The one on the right and the one on the left.
And they hardly ever see the one in the middle.
The little one, the one who's still going to school.
And who walks.

Lost in her sisters' skirts.
And they willingly believe that it's the two older ones who drag the
    youngest along by the hand.
In the middle.
Between them.
To make her walk this rocky path of salvation.
They are blind who cannot see otherwise.
That it's she in the middle who leads her older sisters along.
And that without her they wouldn't be anything.
But two women already grown old.
Two elderly women.
Wrinkled by life.

It's she, the little one, who carries them all.
Because Faith sees only what is.
But she, she sees what will be.
Charity loves only what is.
But she, she loves what will be.

Faith sees what is.
In Time and in Eternity.
Hope sees what will be.
In time and for eternity.

In the future, so to speak, of eternity itself.

Charity loves what is.
In Time and in Eternity.
God and neighbor.
As Faith sees.
God and creation.
But Hope loves what will be.
In time and for eternity.

In the future, so to speak, of eternity.

Hope sees what has not yet been and what will be.
She loves what has not yet been and what will be.

In the future of time and of eternity.

On the *uphill path, sandy and troublesome.*[7]
On the uphill road.
Dragged along, hanging from the arms of her two older sisters,
Who hold her by the hand,
The little hope.
Pushes on.
And in between her two older sisters she seems to let herself be carried.
Like a child who lacks the energy to walk.
And is dragged along the road in spite of herself.
But in reality it is she who moves the other two.
And who carries them,
And who moves the whole world.
And who carries it.
Because no one ever works except for children.

And the two older ones don't walk except for the youngest.

My three virtues, says God.
Master of the Three Virtues.
My three virtues are no different than men and women in their homes.
Children are never the ones who work.
But no one ever works except for children.
It's never the child who goes to the field, who tills and who sows, and
        who reaps and who harvests the grapes and who trims the vine
        and who fells the trees and who cuts the wood.
For winter.
To warm the house in winter.
But would the father have the heart to work if he didn't have his
        children.
If it weren't for the sake of his children.
And in winter when he works hard.
In the forest.[8]
When he works the hardest.
With his billhook and with his saw and with his felling axe and with
        his hand axe.
In the icy forest.

THE PORTAL OF THE MYSTERY OF HOPE

In winter when the snakes sleep in the woods because they're frozen.
And when a bitter North wind blows.
That cuts to his bones.
That passes through each of his limbs.
And he's completely numb and his teeth are chattering.
And the frost makes icicles in his beard.
All of a sudden he thinks about his wife who stayed at home.
About his wife who is such a good homemaker.
Whose husband he is before God.
And about his children who are peaceful and safe at home.
Who are playing and having fun right now in front of the fire.
And who might be fighting.
Together.
For fun.
They pass before his eyes, in a flash before his mind's eye, before his
    soul's eye.
They live in his memory and in his heart and in his soul and in his
    soul's eye.
They live in his gaze.
In a flash he sees his three children playing and laughing in front of
    the fire.
His three children, two boys and a girl.
Whose father he is before God.
The eldest, his boy who was twelve in September.
His daughter who was nine in September.
And his youngest who was seven in June.[9]
So his daughter is in the middle.
Just as it should be.
So that her two brothers can defend her.
In life.
One ahead of her and one behind.
His three children who will succeed him and who will survive him.
On earth.
Who will have his house and his land.
And if he doesn't have a house and land, who will at least have his
    tools.
(If he doesn't have a house and land they won't have them either.
That's just how it is.)

(He has gotten by without them.
They will do as he did. They will work.)
His hand axe and his felling axe and his billhook and his saw.
And his hammer and his file.
And his shovel and his pickaxe.
And his spade for digging the earth.
And if he doesn't have a house and land.
If they don't inherit his house and his land.
At least they will inherit his tools.
His good tools.
That served him so often.
That have grown to fit his hand.
That have so often dug the same earth.
His tools, from use, have made his hands callous and shiny.
But he also, from using them, he made the handles of his tools all
    polished and shiny.
At the handles of his tools his sons will gain, his sons will inherit, the
    hardness of his hands.
But also their skill, their great skill.
Because he is a good worker and a good woodcutter.
And a good vine-grower.
And with his tools his sons will inherit, his children will inherit.
What he has given them, which no one can take away.
(Practically not even God.)
(God has given so much to man.)
The strength of his name, the strength of his blood.
Because they came from him.
And they are sons of France and of Lorraine.[10]
Children of good stock and a good house.
And good blood will show itself.
Children of a good mother.
And above all, what is above everything, with his tools and with his
    ancestry and with his blood his children will inherit.
What is worth more than a house and a piece of land to leave to one's
    children.
Because the house and the land are perishable and will perish.
And the house and the land are exposed to the winter wind.
To this bitter North wind that blows in the forest.

But God's blessing isn't blown by any wind.
What is worth more than tools, what is more industrious and
          hardworking than tools.
What does more work than tools.
And tools end up worn out anyway.
Like man.
What is worth more, what is more durable than lineage and blood.
Even.
Because the line itself and blood are perishable and will perish.
Except the blood of Jesus.
Which will be shed through centuries of centuries.[11]
And the line itself and blood are exposed to the winter wind.
And there could be a winter of descendants.
With his house maybe if he has one and his land.
With his tools certainly and his ancestry and his blood, his children
          will inherit.
What is above everything.
God's blessing, which is on his house and on his ancestors.
The grace of God, which is worth more than anything.
He can be sure of this.
Which is on the poor man and on the working man.
And on him who raises his children well.
He can be sure of this.
Because God promised it.
And because he is supremely faithful in his promises.

His three children who are growing so much.
Provided they don't get sick.
And who will certainly be bigger than he is.
(How proud he is of this in his heart.)
And his two boys will be awfully strong.
His two boys will replace him, his children will take his place on earth.
When he is no longer here.
His place in the parish and his place in the forest.
His place in the church and his place in the house.
His place in the town and his place in the vineyard.
And on the plains and on the hill and in the valley.
His place in Christianity. After all.

His place as man and his place as Christian.
His place as parishioner, his place as worker.
His place as farmer.
His place as father.
His place as a son of Lorraine and of France.
Because these are the places, great God, that must be taken.
And all of this must go on.
When he is no longer here as he is now.
If not get better.
The work around the farm must go on.
And the vine and the wheat and the harvest and the vintage.
And the tilling of the soil.
And the pasturing of the animals.
When he is no longer here as he is now.
If not get better.
Christianity must go on.
The Church militant.
And for that you need Christians.
Always.
France and Lorraine must go on.
Long after he's gone.
As well as they are now.
If not better.
He thinks tenderly of the time when he will be no longer and his
    children will take his place.
On earth.
Before God.
Of that time when he will be no longer and when his children will be.
And when they say his name in town, when they talk about him, when
    his name gets brought up, at some chance remark, it will no
    longer be him that they talk about but his sons.
All together, it will be him and it will not be him, since it will be his
    sons.
It will be his name and it will no longer be and it will not be his
    name, since it will be (will have become) his sons' name.
And he is proud of it in his heart and he thinks about it with such
    tenderness.
That he will no longer be himself but his sons.

THE PORTAL OF THE MYSTERY OF HOPE

And that his name will no longer be his name but his sons' name.
That his name will no longer be at his service but at his sons' service.
Who will bear the name honestly before God.
Openly and proudly.
As he does.
Better than he.
And when they say his name, it's his son they'll be calling, it's his son
      they'll be talking about.
He'll have long been in the cemetery.
Around the church.
He, that is, his body.
Side by side with his fathers and the fathers of his fathers.
Lined up with them.
With his father and his grandfather that he knew.
And with everyone else, all those that he didn't know.
All the men and women of his lineage.
All the old men and all the old women.
His ancestors and forefathers.
And his foremothers.
As many of them as there have been since the parish was founded.
By some founding saint.
Sent by Jesus.
His body, because his soul he will have a long time ago.
Commended to God.
Putting it under the protection of his patron saints.

He will sleep, his body will thus rest.
Among his own, (awaiting his own).
Awaiting the resurrection of the body.
Until the resurrection of the body his body will thus rest.

He thinks tenderly of the time when he will no longer be needed.
And when things will go on all the same.
Because there will be others.
Who will bear the same responsibilities.
And who will perhaps, and who will undoubtedly, bear them better.

He thinks tenderly of the time when he will be no longer.

Because you can't be forever, can you.
You can't be and have been.
And when everything will go on all the same.
When they will not go any worse.
On the contrary.
When things will only go better.
On the contrary.
Because his children will be there, for a while.

His children will do better than he, of course.
And the world will go better.
Later.
He's not jealous of it.
On the contrary.
Nor for having come to the world, as he did, in an ungrateful time.
And to have no doubt prepared for his sons a time that is perhaps less
        ungrateful.
What madman would be jealous of his sons and of the sons of his sons.

Doesn't he work solely for his children.

He thinks tenderly of the time when people will scarcely ever think of
        him except because of his children.
(If they only think about him occasionally. Rarely.)
When his name resounds (warmly) in town, it'll be because someone is
        calling his son Marcel or his son Pierre.
It'll be because someone needs his son Marcel or his son Pierre.
And is calling them, happy to see them. And is looking for them.
Because it's they who will rule then and who will bear the name.
It's they who will rule with their peers, those from the same generation.
It's they who will reign on the face of the earth.
Perhaps for some time still, an old man who remembers
Will say.
Those two Sévin boys are good boys.
It's not surprising.
It runs in the family.
Their father was such a good man.
And after a while the young will repeat with confidence:

The old man was such a good man.
But already they'll know nothing about it.
They'll no longer know then, and the comment itself, the very remark
    will disappear.
He thinks tenderly about the time when he will no longer be even a
    remark.
It's to this end, it's for this that he works, because doesn't one always
    work for one's children.

He'll be nothing but a corpse in six feet of earth under six feet of earth
    under a cross.
But his children will be.
He tenderly greets the new time when he will be no longer.
When he will have ceased to be.
When his children will be.
The reign of his children.

He thinks tenderly of the time that will no longer be his time.
But his children's time.
His children's reign (of time) on earth.
In that time, when they say *The Sévins* it won't be he but they.
Nothing more, without explanation.

His children will bear the name Sévin.
    Or the name Chénin, or the name Jouffin, or Damrémont, or any
        other name from Lorraine.[12]
Any other Christian name, or French name, any name from Lorraine.

At the thought of his children who will have become men and women.
At the thought of his children's time, of his children's reign
On earth,
In their turn,
A tenderness, a warmth, a pride swells in his breast.
(My God, could that be Pride.[13]
But God will forgive him.)
How strong and brave his sons will be in the forest, great God.
Boys as solid as oaks.
In the forest when the winter wind blows.

The bitter north wind.
That will cut to their bones.
And make icicles in their beards.

He laughs when he thinks what they'll look like.
He laughs to himself and perhaps even openly.
Out loud.

When he thinks what they'll look like when they have beards.

And he thinks tenderly about his daughter who will be such a good
        homemaker.
Because she'll certainly be like her mother.
As for him, it's understood, he'll be no longer.
He'll have lost the taste for bread.[14]
But there will be others, great God there will be others,
One must hope,
Who already know the taste for bread and who will know how to bite
        into a good crust of bread.
Who will eat heartily.
Their daily bread.
Who will eat heartily their daily bread and their eternal bread.
(They'll manage very well without him, and he'll no longer sit at table,
        because one must get up from the table when the newcomers
        arrive and nudge one aside.)
There will be others — his children who will live and who will die
        after him if all proceeds in the right order.
And whom he'll see again in heaven.

There will be others, thank God:
France must go on.
Neither France, nor Christianity, nor Lorraine will come to a standstill.
And the parish will not come to a standstill.
Nor will the wheat or the vine.

It's right that the father die before the children.
He thinks about them, by God's grace, and immediately the blood
        rushes to his heart.

And warms him so.

And floods back into all of his limbs, to the very tips of his fingers.

So much it's as if he'd drunk a good glass of Meuse wine.

From the hills above Cepoy.

And the numbness that he had in his fingers, (and he had blown on his hands in vain).

Disappears as if by magic.

And he's left with a shiver of warmth in the tips of his fingers.

And the bitter north wind.

That's still blowing.

Because it doesn't have any children.

Because it's not alive.

And knows nothing about these sorts of things.

The bitter north wind in the forest.

Has just now frozen two big tears that fell stupidly upon his cheeks.

In the sunken furrows of his cheeks, and were just swallowed by his bushy beard.

Like two icicles.

There he is, laughing and ashamed.

Laughing to himself and ashamed both inwardly and outwardly.

And even laughing out loud.

Because it is sweet and it is shameful to cry.

For a man.

So the poor man tries to be discreet.

Pretends that he wasn't just crying.

People always try to be discreet.

And so he looks around, trying not to seem like he's looking to see if someone is looking.

If someone saw him.

By chance.

Laughing to himself and under his breath.

He hurries to wipe those two tears from his cheeks.

And to brush them away.

He swallows and licks his lips with his tongue.

The salty water of his tears at the corners of his lips.

That ran through his beard.

And so he takes his hand, and clumsily.

Awkwardly.

Slyly.

Lowers it to his face.

And with the back of his thumb, he hurries to brush away his tears and
the trace of his tears.

So that no one notices.

So that no one sees that he cried.

And so that no one will have anything to tease him about in town.

Because it's not good for a man to cry.

And his wife who stayed home today.

But who otherwise usually goes to the fields too.

Who is such a good homemaker.

And such a good Christian.

Would she be as willing to work.

And do the housework.

If she weren't working for her children.

Thus, without exception, all the world works for the little girl hope.

All that we do we do for children.

And it's the children who make it all get done.

All that we do.

As if they led us by the hand.

Thus all that we do, everything that everyone does is done for the sake
of the little girl hope.

All that is small is what is most beautiful and greatest.

All that is new is what is most beautiful and greatest.

And baptism is the sacrament for the little ones.

And baptism is the newest sacrament.

And baptism is the sacrament that begins.

All that begins has a character that is never again recovered.

A strength, a novelty, a freshness like dawn.

A youth, an ardor.

A spirit.

A naiveté.

A birth that is never again recovered.

The first day is the most beautiful day.

THE PORTAL OF THE MYSTERY OF HOPE

The first day is perhaps the only beautiful day.
And baptism is the sacrament of the first day.
And baptism is all that is beautiful and great.
Excepting the sacrifice.
And consumption of the body of Our Lord.

There is, in that which begins, a spring; roots that never return.
A departure, a childhood that is not recovered, that is never again
      recovered.
Now, the little girl hope
Is she who forever begins.

This birth.
Perpetual birth.
This childhood.
Perpetual childhood.
What would we do, what would we be, my God, without children.
      What would become of us.
And her two older sisters know well that without her they would be
      but servants of the moment.
Just old maids in a thatched hut.
In a dilapidated shack decaying ever more by the day.
Wearing out with time.
Just old women growing old all alone, growing bored in their hovel.
Women without children.
A dying race.

But instead with her they know well that they are two generous women.
Two women with a future.
Two women who have something to do in life.
And that through this little girl that they're raising they hold all of time
      and eternity itself in the palms of their hands.

Thus it is the children who do nothing.
Those mischievous kids, they pretend that they're doing nothing,
Those sly little children.
They understand what they're doing,
The innocent ones.

The innocent, their hands shall be filled.[15]
That's how it is.
They know well that they do everything; and more than everything;
With their innocent manner;
Seeming not to be aware of anything;
Not to know;
Because it's for them that we work.
In reality.
Because no one ever works except for them.
And nothing gets done except for their sake.

And because all that is made in the world is made only for them.
This is where they get that look of confidence.
So pleasant to see.
That sincere gaze, that gaze which is unbearable to meet and which,
        itself, bears all gazing.
So sweet, so pleasant to watch.
That unbearable gaze.
That sincere gaze, that honest gaze that they have, that sweet gaze
        come straight from heaven.
That's where they get that brow that they have.
That confident brow.
That straight brow, that domed brow, that firm brow, that raised brow.
That confidence that they have.
And it is the very confidence.
Of hope.

Their domed brow, all freshly washed and clean from baptism.
From the waters of baptism.[16]

And their words and that voice so gentle, and together so confident.
So sweet to hear, so young.
That voice from heaven.
For it carries a promise, a secret inward confidence.
Just as their youthful gaze bears a promise, a secret inward confidence,
        and their brow and their whole person.
Their tiny, their noble, their so reverent and reverend person. . . .

Happy children; happy father.
Happy hope.
Happy childhood. Their whole little body, their whole little person, all
their little gestures are full, stream with, overflow with a
certain hope.
Shine with, overflow with an innocence.
Which is the very innocence of hope.

Confidence, unique innocence.
Confidence, inimitable innocence.
The ignorance of a child, the innocence next to which sanctity itself,
the purity of the saint is nothing but filth and decay.
Confidence, ignorance, innocence of heart.
Youthfulness of heart.
Hope; infancy of the heart.
Sweet children, inimitable children, little siblings of Jesus.
Young children.
Children next to whom the greatest of saints are nothing but old age
and decay.

Children, it is for this that you are the masters and that you command
the households.
We understand why.
One glance, one word from you bends the hardest of heads.
You are the masters and this we know well.
You are all children Jesus.
And what man, what madman, what blasphemer would dare to call
himself an adult Jesus.
What saint, even the greatest of them, would dare even to think it.

And you yourselves know well that you are the masters of the house.
Your voice says it, your eyes say it, and your locks of hair, and your
mischievous expressions.
And when you ask for something, you ask like one who laughs because
he's so sure of getting it.

You know well that you will get it.

On the imitation of Jesus.[17] You children imitate Jesus.
You don't imitate him. You *are* children Jesus.
Without being aware of it, without noticing it, without seeing it.
And you know it well.
And man, what man, what saint, even the greatest of them, is not
        aware that he is infinitely far from Jesus.
In his imitation.

The irreparable loss, descent, fall, inevitable despoilment of life.
Which is existence and life and aging itself.
In our childhood we are joined with Jesus.
And as we get older we are disjoined from him, we disjoin ourselves
        from everything throughout our life.

Children, your ignorance, your confidence, your innocence is the very
        ignorance and is the same innocence of Jesus, of the child Jesus.
And his timid confidence.
You are little hopes like the child Jesus was hope.
Truly you are children Jesus.

It is for this, children, that we are so happy, it is for this that you are
        the masters and that you command the households.
It is the very commandment of hope.
Your reign is hope's own reign.

Because the rest of us men, what are we.
In our poor imitation.

And your commandment is the same commandment of Jesus.

Strange lot, strange fate, man's destiny.
When we are children, we are children Jesus, we are joined with the
        child Jesus.
And when we are adults, and disjoined, what are we.

Beautiful children, your gaze is the very gaze of Jesus.
Your blue gaze.
Of the child Jesus.

Your beautiful gaze.
Your brow is the very brow of Jesus.
Your voice is the very voice of Jesus.

And as for us, what are we.
With our veiled gaze.
With our veiled brow.
With our veiled voice.
The edges of our lips curled with bitterness.
And, at best, curled with contrition.
We may never be anything but a recovered innocence.
And they are the first innocence.

What is becoming of us.
What has become of us.
What do we know.
What are we capable of.
What are we doing.
What do we have.
We never have anything but a repaired innocence.
And they have the first innocence.
And in thinking it best, in doing our best with it, in making the best
        of it, we would never be anything more than preserved
        innocence.
But they are the first innocence.
And as much as ripened fruit, perfectly ripened, just picked from the
        tree, is superior to preserved fruit.
Fresh fruit is worth more than preserved fruit.
That's how much a child's innocence is superior to the innocence of an
    · adult.
Is worth more than that which an adult no longer dares even to call his
        innocence.

He thinks about his three children who are at this very moment
        playing in front of the fire.
Are they playing, are they working, who knows.
With children.
Are they working with their mother.

Who can ever tell.
Children are not like adults.
For children playing, working, resting, stopping, running, it's all one.
Together.
It's the same.
They don't make the distinction.
They're happy.
They have fun all the time.
As much when they work as when they play.
They don't even notice it.
They're very happy.
And their commandment is the same commandment of Jesus.
Of the child Jesus.
Hope, too, is she who is always playing.

He thinks about his three children who are playing right now in front
       of the fire.
Just as long as they're happy.
Isn't that all a father could ask.
We live for them, we ask only that our children be happy.

He thinks about his three children whom he explicitly placed under the
       special protection of the Blessed Virgin.
One day when they were sick.[18]
And when he was very much afraid.
He still shudders at the thought of that day.
When he was so scared.
For them and for himself.
Because they were sick.
He was shaking all over because of them.
At the mere idea that they were sick.
He knew very well that he couldn't bear to live like that.
With sick children.
And his wife who was so afraid.
So terribly afraid.
That she just stared straight ahead and knitted her brow and didn't say
       a single word.
Like a wounded animal.

That keeps itself silent.
Because she was feeling the pangs of anguish.
Her throat constricted like a woman being strangled.
Her heart in a vice.
Her fingers around her throat; like the teeth of a vice.
His wife who clenched her teeth, who tightened her lips.
And who spoke rarely and with some other voice.
With a voice that was not her own.
Because she was so terribly afraid.
And didn't want to admit it.
But he, by God, he was a man. He wasn't afraid to speak.
He understood perfectly well that things couldn't go on like that.
Things couldn't continue.
Like that.
He couldn't bear to live with sick children.
So he tried something (something audacious), he still laughs when he
      thinks about it.
He was even somewhat proud of himself. And there certainly was good
      reason for it. And he still shudders from it.
You'd have to say that he was pretty bold and that it was a bold idea.
And yet all Christians could do as much.
You've even got to wonder why they don't.
Just as you would pick up three children and put the three of them.
Together. At the same time.
For fun. Like a game.
In the arms of their mother and their nanny who laughs.
And who cries out.
Because you've given her too many.
And because she's not strong enough to carry them.
So he, brave like a man.
He had taken them, he had taken them into prayer.
(France must, Christianity must go on.)
His three children in sickness, in the misery where they lay.
And he had peacefully given them to you.
In prayer he had given them to you.
Placed very peacefully within the arms of she who bears all of the
      world's sufferings.
And whose arms are already so full.

Because the Son has taken away all sins.
But the Mother has taken away all suffering.

He had said, in prayer he had said, *I can't take anymore. I don't*
understand anything anymore. I've had it up to here.
I no longer want anything to do with it.
It has nothing to do with me.
(France must, Christianity must go on.)
Take them. I give them to you. Do with them what you will.
I've had enough.
She who was the mother of Jesus Christ is also quite capable of being the
mother of these two little boys and this little girl.
Who are the siblings of Jesus Christ.
And for whom Jesus Christ came into the world.
What would this matter to you. You who hold so many others.
What would it matter, one more, one less.
You who held the little Jesus. You who held so many others.
(He meant all the children of men, through centuries of centuries, all
the little siblings of Jesus, and she has held so many through
centuries of centuries.)
People would have to have some nerve, to speak thus.
To the Blessed Virgin.
Tears at the edge of his lashes, words at the edge of his lips, he spoke
thus, in prayer he spoke thus.
Inwardly.
He had such a fit of anger, God forgive him, he still shudders from it
(but he is awfully happy to have thought of it).
(The idiot, as if it was he that thought of it, poor soul.)
He spoke in a fit of anger (may God preserve him) and within this
great violence and, within, on the inside of this great anger
and this great violence, with a great devotion.
You see them, he said, *I give them over to you. And I'm turning my back*
and I'm running away so that you don't give them back to me.
I don't want any more to do with it. You can see for yourself.
How he pats himself on the back for having had the courage to pull
such a stunt.
Not just anyone would have dared.
He was happy. He congratulated himself for it, laughing and trembling.

(He hadn't told his wife about it.
He hadn't dared. Women are sometimes jealous.
It's much better not to make such a fuss over it.
And to have peace in the home.[19]
He arranged things all by himself.
It's more sure that way. And there's more peace.)
Ever since that time everything has been going well.
Naturally.
How would you expect it to go otherwise.
Than well.
Because it was the Blessed Virgin who was involved.
Who took on the responsibility.
And she knows better than we do.

And yet She, who had taken them, she had already held so many
          before these three.
(He had done something unique.
Why don't all Christians do it?)
He had been awfully brave.
But Nothing ventured, nothing gained.
It is only the most faint-hearted who lose.
It's really curious that all Christians don't do as much.
It's so simple.
It's always the simple things that get overlooked.
We'll search and search, and hurt ourselves searching, and we'll never
          think of what is simplest.
Ultimately, we're all dumb, may as well admit it immediately.

And yet She, who had taken them, she was never short on children.
She had had others before these three, she will have others, she had
          others afterwards.
She had had others, she will have others through centuries of centuries.

And She, who had taken them, he knew for sure that she would take
          them.
She wouldn't have had the heart to leave them orphans.
(All the same, what a coward he had been.)
She couldn't have just left them by the gate.

(He had counted on that,
the rogue.)
She had been forced to take them,
She who had taken them.
He's still pleased with himself.

And yet we are so proud of having children.
(But men are not jealous.)
And watching them eat and watching them grow.
And, at night, watching them sleep like angels.
And giving them a kiss in the morning and at night, and at noon.
Right on the crown of their heads.[20]
When they bow their head innocently like a colt lowering its head.
As supple as a colt, as playful as a colt.
As supple in their neck and the nape of their neck. And in their whole
    body and in their back.
As the supple and growing stem of a vigorous plant.
A young plant.
As the very stem of growing hope.
They bend their back laughing like a young, like a beautiful colt, and
    their neck, and the nape of their neck and their whole head.
To present themselves to their father, for their father's kiss right on the
    crown of their head.
The center of their hair, the birth-place, the source, the point of origin
    of their hair.
That point, right on the crown of their head, that center around which
    their strands of hair turn, in circles, in a spiral.
They enjoy that.
(They always enjoy themselves.)
They make a game of it. They make a game out of everything.
They hum, they sing songs that we've never heard and that they make
    up as they go along, they sing constantly.
And with the same movement, they turn themselves around, only
    barely stopping.
Like a young stem that balances itself in the wind and then returns to
    its natural movement.
For them, their father's kiss is a game, an amusement, a ceremony.
A greeting.

Something taken for granted, something very good, without
    importance.
A simple little thing.
Something they don't even particularly notice.
Which is as much to say.
It's become such a habit.
It's just something they're owed.
Their heart is pure.
They receive it like a morsel of bread.
They play, they have fun with it like a morsel of bread.
Their father's kiss. It's their daily bread. If they only knew what it
    meant to their father.
Poor children. But that's none of their business.
They'll have plenty of time to learn about that later.
For now they only know, when their eyes meet their father's gaze.
That he doesn't seem to be enjoying himself enough.
In life.

And children when they cry.
It's infinitely ever-better[21] than we when we laugh.
Because they cry in hope.
And we laugh only in faith and in love.

He thus put his children in a safe place and he's happy and laughs to
    himself and he even laughs out loud and rubs his hands.
Because of the great trick he played.
I mean because of the great plan that he thought up. That he carried
    out.
(It's also because he couldn't endure it any longer.)
He placed his children safe within the arms of the Blessed Virgin.
And he went away with arms free.

He went away with his hands empty.
He who had given them over.
Like a man who was carrying a basket.
And who couldn't hold it anymore and whose shoulders were
    beginning to ache.
And who set his basket on the ground.

Or handed it over to someone else.

It's the opposite of a man who hires out his children to a farm.
Because he who hires out his children to a farm.
He remains the owner of his children.
And it's the farmer who becomes their borrower. The farmer.
He, likewise, no longer wished to be anything but the borrower of his
      children.
From now on he only receives the fruits of his children.
And it's God himself who has responsibility for them (and receives
      their fruits) as their owner.
But the good God is a good owner.

Admire the wisdom of this man.[22]
This man who no longer wished to be anything but the borrower of
      his children.
This man who goes away, who leaves with hands empty.
Because God is not jealous, nor is the Blessed Virgin.
They peacefully leave all the joy of his children to him.
It's nice to have God as the owner.
He's clever, this man, he placed his children back in the arms of the
      Blessed Virgin, in the hands of God.
Of God their creator.
Isn't all of creation in God's hands.
Isn't all of creation God's property.

Children when they cry are happier than we are when we laugh.
And when they're sick they're more unhappy than anyone.
And more touching.
Because we feel and they do too that it's already
A lessening of their childhood.
And the first sign of their growing old.
Toward death.
A temporal death.

And she, who had taken them, she was
So touching and so beautiful. (While he went away with a light heart.)

And she, who had taken them, she was
So touching and so pure.
Not just filled with faith and filled with love.
But filled with hope itself.
Pure and young like hope. (While he went away with arms free.)

And she, who had taken them, she was
In her tender youth. (While he went away with hands empty.)

And she, who had taken them, she was
In her youth eternal.

There are days in life when you feel that patron saints are not enough.
Not to offend anyone.
(And she, who had taken them, she had so many family
         responsibilities.)
You feel that patron saints no longer suffice.
(Not to offend them.)
There's some great danger and you've got to go higher up.
It's better to deal with the good God than with his saints.[23]
(And she, who had taken them, she was
So touching and so pure.
Mater Dei, mother of God,
Mother of Jesus and of all his brothers and sisters.
Jesus' siblings.)
You've got to go directly to the good God and to the Blessed Virgin.
(And she, who had taken them, she had
So many children in her arms.
All the children of men.
From the first little one she had carried in her arms.
The little man who laughed like a jewel.
And who ever since had caused her so much anguish.
Because he died for the salvation of the world.)
And she, who had taken them, she was
So ardent and so pure. There are days when you really feel that you
         can't content yourself with ordinary saints.
When ordinary saints no longer suffice. And she, who had taken them,
         she was

So young and so powerful.
So powerful next to God.
So powerful next to the All-Powerful.

And she, who had taken them, she was
So burdened with suffering.
And she had seen so much of it ever since the little boy.
Who would laugh while nursing.
Because it has been a long time since she was the mother of the Seven
      Sufferings.
The seven sufferings were just the beginning.
And for a while now she has been and we have made her
The mother of the seven and of the seventy times seven sufferings.

While he, who had handed them over, he went away with an easy
      mind and clear vision.
Like a man who has taken a long walk.
Carefree, his frown gone, and brow smoothed over.
His brow unknit.
Like a man who's just escaped from the greatest of all dangers.
And she, who had taken them, she was
So eternally full of cares.
And she had taken them into her guardianship and into her care.
(After so many others, with so many others.)
And keeps them for eternity.

And thus she who is not only
All faith and all love.
But who is also all hope.
And that is seven times more difficult.
Just as it is also seven times more full of grace.
Thus she has taken, into her care and into her guardianship,
And keeps for eternity,
The young virtue Hope.

You've got to be honest. St. Marcel is still quite a great saint.
And quite a great patron.

(Even though we can't be sure what he did exactly. But we don't have
       to talk about that.
And perhaps there were even more than one.
But in any event he was a great saint, let's even say just a saint, that's
       already a lot.)[24]
But there are days when you have to go higher up.

You can't be afraid to tell the truth. St. Germaine is still quite a great
       saint.
And quite a great patron. And who must be rather powerful.
(Even though we can't be sure what she did exactly. But we don't have
       to talk about that.)
But what difference does it make, she's done at least enough to be a
       saint and a great saint. And that's already a lot.
That's already everything.
To be merely a saint, that's already everything.
And there's also her comrade St. Germain, who might do, born in
       Auxerre, bishop of Auxerre, who will possess the eternal glory.
Of having consecrated to God our great saint and our great patron *and
       our great friend.*
St. Geneviève.
Who was a simple shepherdess.

St. Germain, called *the Auxerrois,* born in Auxerre, bishop of Auxerre,
Bishop and saint in the times of the barbarian armies,
Bishop and saint of France.
And who might be helpful as a patron.
As a very great patron.

And this St. Geneviève, born in Nanterre.
Parisian, patroness of Paris.
Patroness and saint of France, these are some great patrons and great
       saints.
St. Marcel, St. Germain, St. Geneviève.
Yet there are days when the greatest of friendships are not enough.
Neither Marcel nor Geneviève.
Our great friend, Geneviève.
Nor the greatest of patronages nor the greatest of sanctities.

There are days when patrons and saints are not enough.
The greatest of patrons and the greatest of saints.
Ordinary patrons, ordinary saints.
And you have to keep climbing, higher and higher; always climbing,
    higher still.

Up to the ultimate sanctity, the ultimate purity, the ultimate beauty,
    the ultimate patronage.
You must have the courage to tell the truth. St. Peter is a great saint
    and a great patron among all the patrons.
(We know very well what he did, this one, but it's probably better not
    to talk too much about it.)[25]
But he is without doubt a very great patron.
Because he was the cornerstone.
And the Gates of Hell shall not prevail against it.
Tu es Petrus, et super hanc petram.
And he is Peter for eternity and upon this rock.
And for the person who wishes to enter Heaven, he is the greatest
    patron that anyone could come up with.
Because he stands at the gate and he holds the gate and he is the
    gatekeeper and he has the keys.
He is the eternal Gatekeeper and the eternal Keybearer.
He wears at his belt the great ring of keys.
And yet I swear to you he is not a prison guard.
Because he is the guardian of Freedom eternal.
And in a prison, from a prison, the prisoners would very much like to
    escape.
But in heaven, on the other hand, those who are in paradise are not
    ready to leave.
There's no danger that they'll ask to leave.
You'd have to pay them a lot to make them leave.
They wouldn't want to give their places to someone else.

That's why you couldn't find a better patron than St. Peter.

But there comes a day, there comes a time.
There comes a moment when St. Marcel and St. Germaine.
And St. Germain himself and our great friend the great St. Geneviève.

THE PORTAL OF THE MYSTERY OF HOPE

And the great St. Peter himself is no longer enough.
And you must resolutely do what you've got to do.

And so you must gather your courage with both hands.
And address yourself directly to she who is above them all.
Be bold. Just once. Address yourself boldly to she who is infinitely
        beautiful.
Because she's also infinitely good.

To she who intercedes.
The only one who can speak with the authority of a mother.
Address yourself boldly to she who is infinitely pure.
Because she's also infinitely gentle.

To she who is infinitely noble.
Because she's also infinitely gracious.
Infinitely courteous.
Courteous like the priest who at the threshold of the church goes to
        meet the newborn at the threshold.
On the day of his baptism.
To introduce him into the house of God.

To she who is infinitely rich.
Because she's also infinitely poor.

To she who is infinitely lofty.
Because she's also infinitely lowly.

To she who is infinitely great.
Because she's also infinitely small.
Infinitely humble.
A young mother.

To she who is infinitely righteous.
Because she's also infinitely yielding.

To she who is infinitely joyful.
Because she's also infinitely sorrowful.

Seven and seventy times seven times sorrowful.
To she who is infinitely moving.
Because she's also infinitely moved.

To she who is all Grandeur and all Faith.
Because she's also all Love.

To she who is all Faith and all Love.
Because she's also all **Hope**.

Fortunately the saints are not jealous of each other.
That would be overdoing it.
It would be a bit much.
And altogether it's fortunate that they're not jealous of the Blessed
      Virgin.
It's what we call the communion of saints.
They understand what she is and that as much as the child surpasses
      the man in purity.
That's as much and seventy times more that she surpasses them in
      purity.

As much as the child surpasses the man in youth.
That's as much and seventy times more that she surpasses the saints
      (even the greatest of saints), in youth and childlikeness.

As much as the child surpasses the man in hope.
That's as much and seventy times more that she surpasses the saints
      (even the greatest of saints), in faith, in love, in **hope**.

Man is nothing next to the child in purity, in youthfulness, in hope.
In childlikeness.
In innocence.
In ignorance.
In helplessness.
In newness.
Thus, as much, and seventy times more, as the saintly women and
      men, the saintliest women and the saintliest men.
Are nothing next to her in childlikeness and purity.

In innocence and in youthfulness.
In ignorance, in helplessness, in newness.
In faith, in love, in hope.

Geneviève, my child, was a simple shepherdess.
Jesus too was a simple shepherd.
But what a shepherd, my child.
Shepherd of what herd. Pastor of what sheep.
In what country of the world.
Pastor of the hundred sheep that dwelt in the fold, the pastor of the
          lost sheep, pastor of the sheep that returned.[26]
And who, in order to help it return, because its legs could no longer
          carry it,
Its tired legs,
Takes it gently and returns it himself on his shoulders,
Gently draping it around his neck like a laurel,
The sheep's head thus leaning gently against his right shoulder,
Which is the good side,
Against Jesus' right shoulder,
Which is the side for the good ones,
And its body curving all around his collar and around his nape.
Around his neck like a laurel,
Like a woolen scarf that holds in warmth.
So the sheep even keeps his own master warm,
The woolen sheep.
Its two forelegs well and duly held in his right hand,
Which is the good side,
Held and gripped tight,
Gently but firmly,
Its two hind legs well and duly held in his left hand,
Gently but firmly,
Like you would carry a child piggyback.
Over your two shoulders,
His right leg in your right hand, his left leg in your left hand.
Thus the Savior, thus the good pastor, which means the good shepherd,
Carries this sheep on piggyback, the sheep that was lost, that was going
          to get lost
So that the stones in the path wouldn't bruise its bruised feet.

Because there will be more joy in heaven over one sinner who returns,
Than for a hundred righteous ones who never left.
Because the hundred righteous ones who haven't left will have remained.
They will have remained only in faith and in love.
But the sinner who left and who almost became lost
By his very going away, and because he was going to miss the evening
    call
He aroused fear and thus he caused *hope* itself to spring forth from the
    very heart of God,
From Jesus' heart
The shudder of fear and the shiver,
The tremor of hope.

Because of this lost sheep Jesus experienced fear in love.
And the kind of tremor that divine hope creates in love itself.

And God had been afraid he'd have had to condemn it.

By this sheep, and because it wouldn't return to the fold, and because it
    was going to miss the evening call,
Jesus, as a man, came to know human anxiety,
Jesus made man,
He came to know what anxiety is in the very heart of love,
The gnawing anxiety in the worm-eaten heart of love,
But thus he also came to know the very first hint of hope's awakening.
When the young virtue hope begins to rise in the heart of man,
Under the rough bark,
Like the first bud of April.

Thus Geneviève was a shepherdess but Mary
Is the mother of the shepherd himself
And as long as there is a fold,
That is to say a sheepfold,
She is the mother of the eternal shepherd.

And so one day you'll have to go
To she who intercedes.
Beyond Marcel and Germaine and Germain,

THE PORTAL OF THE MYSTERY OF HOPE

Geneviève and St. Peter.
Beyond the patrons, the patronesses, the saints,
Beyond the eternal patroness of Paris.
And even beyond the eternal patron of Rome
You'll have to go
To she who is the most majestic.
Because she is also the most maternal.

To she who is infinitely white.
Because she is also the mother of the Good Shepherd,
    of the Man who hoped.

(And he had good reason to hope, seeing as how he succeeded in
        bringing back the sheep.)

To she who is infinitely celestial.
Because she is also infinitely worldly.

To she who is infinitely eternal.
Because she is also infinitely temporal.

To she who is infinitely above us.
Because she is also infinitely in our midst.

To she who is the mother and the queen of the angels.
Because she is also the mother and the queen of men.
Queen of the heavens, earthly ruler.

(Empress of the infernal swamplands.)[27]

To she who is Mary.[28]
Because she is full of grace.

To she who is full of grace.
Because she is with us.

To she who is with us.
Because the Lord is with her.

To she who intercedes.
Because she is blessed among women.
And blessed is the fruit of her womb, Jesus.

To she who is full of grace.
Because she is full of grace.

To she who is infinitely queen
Because she is the most humble of creatures.
Because she was a poor woman, a miserable woman, a poor Jewess
       from Judea.

To she who is infinitely distant
Because she is infinitely near.

To she who is the highest princess
Because she is the most humble woman.

To she who is the nearest to God
Because she is the nearest to men.

To she who is infinitely saved
Because in her turn she saves infinitely.

To she who is most pleasing to God.

To she who is full of grace
Because she is fully efficacious
Now.

And because she is full of grace and fully efficacious
And at the hour of our death amen.

To have conceived and to have given birth,
To have nourished and to have carried
The Man who feared,
The Man who hoped.

(And he had good reason to hope, seeing as how he succeeded in
        saving so many men and women saints. At least for starters.
    Well, whatever, he succeeded all the same.)

To she who is the only Queen
Because she is the most humble subject.

To she who is the first next to God
Because she is the first among men.

The first among men and women.
The first among sinners.

The first among the men and women saints.
The first among carnal man.

And as well as the first among the angels themselves.

Listen, my child, I'm going to explain to you, listen well, I'll explain
        why,
how, for what reason,
the Blessed Virgin is a unique, a rare creature,
Of an infinite rarity,
Preeminent among all,
Unique among all the creatures.
Try to follow me. I'm not sure if you'll understand.
All of creation was pure. Try to follow me.
(Ultimately Jesus succeeded, you don't have to be too difficult.
You don't have to be too demanding.
Of life.
Because all the same he was able to bring in, to gather this bunch of
        saints.
Which, as he rose, he laid at the feet of his father.
Along with the souls of the just that he had perfumed with his virtues.)
So all of creation was pure.
Just as it had come, just as it had burst forth pure and young and new
        from the hands of its Creator.

But Satan's sin seduced, corrupted half of the angels.
And Adam's sin seduced, corrupted the blood of the whole human race.

Such that only half of the angels were pure.
And nothing of the men.
Not one of the men.
In the whole of creation,
With the native purity, with the young purity, with the first purity,
        with the created purity, with the infant purity, with the purity
        of creation itself.

When it happened that this unique creature was created,
Blessed among women,

Infinitely unique, infinitely rare,
Now.

Infinitely pleasing to God.
And at the hour of our death amen,
Preeminent among all creatures.

When finally, when this unique creature was created one day in time
        for eternity,
For the salvation of the world.
To be the Mother of God.
To be woman and yet to be pure.

Listen well, my child, follow closely, it's hard to explain.
Why it is that she is unique in this respect. But try to follow me.
In all creatures there's something missing.
Not only that they're not the Creator,
Not God their Creator.
(That's in the order of things.
It's order itself.)
That they're not their own Creator.
But besides this they are always lacking something.
What those that are carnal lack is precisely being pure.
This we know.

But what those that are pure lack is precisely being carnal.
This we ought to know.

And she however doesn't lack anything.
Except truly to be God himself.
To be her Creator.
(But this is in the order of things.)

Because being carnal she is pure.
But, being pure, she is also carnal.

And it's for this that she is not only unique among women.
But she's unique among all creatures.

Literally the first after God. After the Creator.
Immediately after.
Just below, the very first step below God.
In the celestial hierarchy.

It was in this disaster. In this flaw. In this lack.
In this disaster where, in half of the angels and in all of the men, there
        was no longer anything carnal that was pure,
With the purity of birth.
When one day this woman was born of the tribe of Judea
For the salvation of the world
Because she was full of grace.

And besides Joseph was of the house of David.
Who was of the house of Jacob.

When she was born so full of her first innocence.
As pure as Eve before the first sin.[29]

*See that you do not harm one of these little ones: indeed I tell you, their
        angels in heaven gaze continually upon the face of my Father, who
        is in heaven.*

Indeed the Son of man has come to save that which had perished.

What do you think? If someone had a hundred sheep, and if one of them
  lost its way;

(Took the wrong path);

wouldn't he leave the ninety-nine in the mountains and go look for the one
  that was lost?

And if he happened to find it: Truly, I tell you, he would rejoice more over
  the one lost sheep than over the ninety-nine that were not lost.

Thus it is not the will of your Father,[30] who is in heaven, that a single one
  of his little ones should be lost.

The Good Pastor, that is, the good shepherd.
Learned anxiety from the lost sheep.
From the sheep who did not remain with the other ninety-nine.
A mortal anxiety.
(The devouring anxiety in the heart of Jesus.)
The anxiety of not finding it. Of not knowing.
Of never recovering it. Human anxiety.
The mortal anxiety of having to condemn it.
But finally he is saved.
The savior himself is saved.
He is saved from having to condemn it.
Now he can breathe again.
That makes it forever one of the saved.
He will never have to condemn this soul.

From this little sheep who merely lost its way,
(That could happen to anyone.)

et erraverit una ex eis,[31]

and it happened to the greatest saints
To follow the way of sin
From this little sheep of a soul, as man, he learned a man's anxiety.

THE PORTAL OF THE MYSTERY OF HOPE

But from this silly little sheep of a soul (which had frightened him so
    terribly), as man, he learned a man's hope.

From this tiny sheep, nothing at all, that was lost,
    from this sheep creature
Man, as man, he came to know the budding of hope,
The budding of hope that awakens in the heart more gently than the
    delicate bud of April.

In all creatures there's something lacking, and not only not being
        Creator.
What those that are carnal lack, as we know, is being pure.
But what we ought to know is that those that are pure lack being
    carnal.
One alone is pure being carnal.
One alone is carnal together with being pure.
It's for this that the Blessed Virgin is not only the greatest blessing ever
    to have fallen to earth.
But even the greatest blessing that ever descended upon the whole of
    creation.
She is not only the first among women.

Blessed among women,[32]

She is not only the first among all creatures,
But she is a unique creature, infinitely unique, infinitely rare.

One alone and no other is both carnal and pure. Because the angels on
        one hand
The angels are certainly pure, but they aren't the least bit carnal.
They have no idea what it is to have a body, *to be* a body.
They have no idea what it is to be a poor creature.
A carnal creature.
A body kneaded from the clay of the earth.
The carnal earth.
They don't understand this mysterious bond, this created bond,
Infinitely mysterious,
Between the soul and the body.

Because God not only created the soul and the body.
The immortal soul and the body that is mortal but will be resurrected.
But he also created, as a third creation he created
This mysterious tie, this created tie,
This attachment, this bond between the body and the soul,
Between spirit and matter,
Between that which is immortal and that which is mortal but will be
        resurrected
And the soul is tied to mud and to ash.
To mud when it rains and to ash when it's dry out.
And yet tied thus the soul must bring its salvation.
Like a good work horse, like a strong and loyal beast, like a great beast
        from Lorraine that pulls the plow.
With its strength and with its energy it must not only drive itself, pull
        itself, drag itself.
Carry itself on its own four feet.
But with the same strength and energy it must also drive and must also
        pull and must also drag the inanimate plow.
Inanimate without it, which would not be able to drive itself all alone,
        pull itself, drag itself all alone.
Drive itself, drag itself, pull itself without the horse.
Inanimate without it but industrious with it, hardworking with it,
        active with it.
Behind the horse this plow tills the soil of Lorraine.
(But tills under one condition, and that's that someone pulls it.)
Just as the work horse, the stout beast must not only carry itself and
        drive itself,
Upon its four legs, upon its four feet,
But also drag the plow which, thus animated, tills the soil behind it,
Thus the soul, this beast of burden, and of an earthly burden,
Of a carnal burden,
Not only must this soul drive itself and carry itself upon its four virtues,
Pull itself and drag itself.
But it must also drive and must also carry,
It must still pull and must still drag
This body thrust into the earth that tills the clod of earth behind it.
This inert body, lifeless without the soul.
Inert without it, industrious with it.

Animated by the soul, the hardworking body is able to till this soil.
Succeeds in tilling it.
Not only must she, the soul, bring her salvation to herself, all for
	herself.
She must also bring her salvation to the body, her own salvation to
	him, the body.[33]
And she must also bring her salvation to him who will be resurrected.
Their common salvation, their double salvation together so that after
	the final judgment,
Immediately after,
Together they will share the eternal, communal happiness,
She, immortal, and he, mortal, the dead but resurrected,
He, having merely become a glorious body.
As two hands joined in prayer,
Where one is no less just than the other,
Thus the body and the soul are like two hands joined.
And both of them together will enter jointly into the eternal life.
And they will be two hands joined together for that which is infinitely
	more than prayer.
And infinitely more than a sacrament.
Or else they will both together fall as two wrists bound
For an eternal captivity.

As a good worker, in order to till this heavy soil,
That clings to the blade of the plow,
Hitches the plow (itself powerful,
But in itself inert),
To the powerful horse,
(And he doesn't put the plow before the horse),
Thus the Lord God, in order to till this carnal soil,
This thick earth that clings to the body and to the heart of man,
This heavy earth,
This earthly earth,
And worldly earth,

(Queen of heaven, earthly ruler),

Thus the Lord God has hitched the body to the soul.

And as it is necessary that the work horse pull for itself and for the
plow,
Likewise it is also necessary that the soul pull for herself and for the
body,
That she bring her salvation, their salvation, for herself and for the
body.
Because neither of the two, neither she nor he, will be saved without
the other.
We don't have any choice. You either have to be two hands joined or
two wrists bound.
Two hands joined that ascend jointly toward happiness.
Two wrists bound that fall bound toward captivity.
Neither will the hands be disjoined nor will the wrists be unbound.
Because God himself has attached the immortal to the mortal.
And to that which is dead but will be resurrected.

This, my child, is what the angels don't understand.
I mean to say that this is what they haven't experienced.
What it is to have this body; to have this bond with this body; to be
this body.
To have this bond with the earth, with this earth, to be this earth, clay
and dust, ash and the mud of the earth,
The very body of Jesus.[34]

Thus the soul must not work only for herself, she must not look out
only for herself.
But she must also work for her servant the body.
Like a rich man who happens to want to cross over a bridge.
He pays the toll collector who has a little hut at the entrance of the
bridge.
He pays a penny for himself and, with it, a penny for his servant who
follows.
Thus, the soul must pay for the soul and the body, it is necessary that
the soul work for the soul and the body.
Because it is always she, the soul, who is a rich man,
And he, the poor body, no matter what he does, no matter what he
says, with all of his pride he will never be anything but a poor
creature.

And it's always he that's wrong.
(Even when he's right.)
Especially when he's right.

This, my child, is what the angels do not understand,
    I mean to say what they have never experienced.

The sins of the flesh and the unique remissions of the flesh.

The sins that are of the flesh and that are of nothing but the flesh.

And that any creature that isn't carnal ignores.
The sins of the flesh and of the earthly earth that the angels only know
        from having heard them talked about.
Like a story from another world.
And almost, as it were, from another creation.

The carnal sins that the angels do not know.
I mean that they haven't experienced.

The sins of the body and of the worldly heart.
(Atoned for by the body and by the heart.)

The sins of the flesh and of the blood.
(Atoned for by the flesh and by the Blood.[35])

The earthly sins.
The worldly sins.
The earthy sins.
The sins of the soil.
And of the earthly earth.

The first carnal sin, when with a sudden burst your blood boils and
        your temples throb, in a burst of anger.
In a movement of anger.
The sin of anger.

The second carnal sin, my child, the greatest sin that has ever been
        seen on earth.
When the blood sinks in your heart, the sin of despair.

And along the path of despair, my child, the greatest temptation that
        has ever been felt on earth.
When the blood trembles and panics within the heart.
The greatest carnal temptation.
But it is certainly a temptation.
The temptation of mortal anxiety.
When the Pastor himself was afraid and trembled in his heart
To have to condemn it, to lose it, I mean to allow the sheep to get
        itself lost.
The mortal fear, the mortal anxiety to have to condemn it to death.
More precisely I mean to say to have to allow it to condemn itself to
        death.
In montibus, in the mountains, when he was afraid he'd never find it
        again.
To be forced
To let it lose itself in the night.
Of eternal death.

The sins of the flesh, but the remissions of the flesh.
They don't know the carnal remissions either.
The infinite remission, both eternal and at one stroke.
And together inseparably temporal and carnal.
When all the sins of the world together and with one stroke
Were ransomed by the placing on the cross of a man's body.
When the thorns from the crown of thorns caused the drops of a man's
        blood to drip down the forehead of his face.
When the four nails in his limbs caused a man's blood to drip *onto* **the
        earth** and onto the wood of the cross.
When the Roman lance, piercing a man's side, caused a man's blood to
        flow down his side.

And preceding this same total remission
This global remission

As the heir apparent in the king's succession precedes the globe of the
empire and of the earth,
And as the child in a procession precedes the Body itself and the Holy
Sacrament,
Preceding every remission, they don't understand that which is almost
sweeter than the remission itself.
So to speak.
When the blood stirs and begins to rise slowly in the heart,
Young hope,
The movement of hope,
When a young blood begins to surge back into the heart.
As the young sap of April that begins to flow, to gush underneath the
rough bark.

What a commandment, what authority, what crushing brutality of
hope.
See that you do not harm a single one of these little ones:
A single one:
Indeed I tell you,
that their angels in heaven
gaze continually upon the face of my Father, who is in heaven.[36]

Just as we see, just as we feel the sap in the month of May
Peep through the rough bark,
So we feel, so we see in the month of Easter
A new blood rise and peep through
The thick skin of our hearts,
Through the skin of anger, through the skin of despair,
Through the thick skin of sin.

That is what they don't understand, not even the greatest carnal sin.
When the blood rises and swells and puffs itself up in our hearts and
in our head.
When in a sudden movement, in a grand movement the blood rises
and swells up
In a stirring of pride.
When the blood, like a beast, jumps, all of a sudden,
Like a bird of prey, like a beast of prey

In a rush of pride.
Pride, the greatest sin that has ever been seen on earth
And in the whole of creation.
Pride of the body, pride of the blood, pride of the flesh.
Which swells and buzzes throughout the body like a buzzing storm.
And which throbs at the temples like the beating of a drum.
Ancient pride, as old as the race, as old as the flesh,
   and like the sap of the silver birch.
Like the sap and the blood of pride, like the sap and the blood of the
     oak
Carnal pride, that's what they don't understand,
What they haven't the slightest experience of.
They of course have had their pride too, I mean those that have fallen.
Because of pride, Lucifer, Satan. Their hellish pride.
But it was a pale pride, a bloodless pride,
A pride of the spirit, a pride of the head,
Not at all a pride of the heart and blood,
Not at all a pride of the body,
Not at all a pride of this earthly
Earth.

It was a pride in thinking, a poor pride of ideas.
A pale pride, a vain pride all in the head.
Smoke.
Not at all a thick and heavy pride nourished by fat and blood.
Brimming with health.
The skin glowing.
And which could only be redeemed by the flesh and blood.

A pride all swollen with blood
That buzzes in your ears
With the buzzing of blood,
A pride that infuses your eyes with blood,
And that beats like a drum in your temples,
That's what they don't understand.

They thus do not understand that there is an Easter
An Easter day, an Easter Sunday

      THE PORTAL OF THE MYSTERY OF HOPE

An Easter week
An Easter month
For the awakening, for the reawakening of carnal hope
Just as, for the sap of the oak and the silver birch, there is
A month of April, a month of May.

They don't know anything about this carnal pride, this full carnal
        pride, this hot carnal pride,
Brought by the boiling of blood.
They thus do not understand the carnal remission
Brought by the shedding of blood.

They don't understand the great pride of man,
So full of himself.
So fat.
So swollen, so fed on himself.
They know nothing about all this fat, all this food
That cannot be atoned for
Except by the fearsome, except by the horrible poverty,
Except by the emaciation
Of Jesus on the cross.

They know nothing about the old royal pride, they know nothing
        about the ancient pride,
The sanguine pride, stuffed with itself, the pride that boils in its skin,
        they thus know nothing about the fact
That the young, that the carnal, that the shy hope
Marches at the head of the line,
Advancing innocently
Because she is the heir apparent of France.

What brutality, my child, what imposition, what violence from God.
What a beating, what a commandment from hope.
See that you do not harm **a single one** *of these little ones:*
Indeed I tell you,
That their angels in heaven gaze continually upon the face of my Father,
Who is in heaven.

Jesus Christ, my child, did not come to tell us tales.
You see, he didn't make this voyage of coming to the earth,
A great voyage, between you and me,
(And he was so comfortable where he was.)
(Before coming.
He didn't have all our worries.)
He didn't make this voyage of descending to the earth
To come recount anecdotes for us
And jokes.
There's no time for fooling around.
He didn't use, he didn't engage, he didn't spend
The thirty-three years of his earthly life,
Of his carnal life,
The thirty years of his private life,
The three years of his public life,
The three days of his passion and of his death,
(And in limbo the three days of his burial),
He didn't use, he didn't engage, he didn't spend all of that,
His thirty years of work and his three years of preaching and his three
          days of his passion and of his death,
His thirty-three years of prayer,
His incarnation, which is really his assumption of the flesh,
His taking on of flesh and of the carnal, his taking on of man and his
          being placed on the cross and his being placed in the tomb,
His in-carnal-ation[37] and his agony,
His life as a man and his life as a worker and his life as a priest and his
          life as a saint and his life as a martyr,
His life as a believer,
His life as Jesus,
In order to come to us afterwards (at the same time) just to spin yarns.
He didn't use, he didn't engage, he didn't spend all of that.
He didn't make such an expense
A considerable expense
In order to come give us, to come give us afterwards
Riddles
To figure out
Like a magician.
Pretending to be clever.

No, no, my child, and Jesus didn't give us dead words either
For us to seal up into little boxes
(Or even big ones.)
And for us to preserve in (some) rancid oil
Like the Egyptian mummies.
Jesus Christ, my child, didn't give us canned words
To keep;
Rather, he gave us living words
To nourish.
Ego sum via, veritas et vita,
I am the way, the truth and the life.[38]
Words of life, living words cannot be preserved except alive,
Nourished alive,
Nourished, carried, warmed, warm in a living heart.
Not at all preserved moldy in little boxes of wood or of cardboard.
As Jesus took, was forced to take a body, to take on flesh,
In order to pronounce these (carnal) words and to have them be
        understood,
So he could pronounce them,
Thus we, similarly we, *in the imitation of Jesus,*
Thus we, who are flesh, we have to take advantage of this,
Take advantage of the fact that we are carnal in order to preserve them,
        in order to warm them up, in order to nourish them in us,
        alive and carnal,
(This is what the angels themselves don't understand, my child, this is
        what they've never experienced.)
As a carnal mother nourishes, and warms at her heart her last-born,
Her carnal infant, at her breast,
Securely held in the fold of her arm,
Thus, taking advantage of the fact that we are carnal,
We must nourish, we have to nourish in our heart,
With our flesh and with our blood,
With our heart,
The carnal Words,
The eternal Words, pronounced carnally in time.
Miracle of miracles, my child, mystery of mysteries.
Because Jesus Christ has become our carnal brother
Because he has pronounced, carnally and in time, eternal words,

In monte,[39] upon the mountain,
It is to us, the weak, that he was given,
He depends on us, weak and carnal,
To bring to life and to nourish and to keep alive in time
These words pronounced alive in time.
Mystery of mysteries, this privilege that was given to us,
This incredible, exorbitant privilege,
To keep alive the words of life,
To nourish with our blood, with our flesh, with our heart
The words which, without us, would collapse fleshless.

To grant, (it's incredible), to grant to the eternal words,
In addition, like a second eternity,
A temporal and carnal eternity, an eternity of flesh and of blood,
Nourishment, an eternity of body,
A worldly eternity.

Thus the words of Jesus, the eternal words are the infants, the living
        infants suckling on our blood and on our heart
On us who live in time.
Like the least of the peasants, if the queen in her palace is unable to
        nourish the heir apparent
Because she lacks milk,
So the least of the peasant women from the least of the parishes might
        be called to the palace,
Given that she'd be a good wet-nurse,
And she might be called to nourish a son of France,
Thus all of us children from all the parishes
We are called to nourish the word of the son of God.

O misery, o misfortune,[40] that this would happen to us,
That it would belong to us, that it would depend on us
To make the word understood through the centuries of centuries,
To make it resound.

O misery, o happiness, that it would depend on us,
Shivers of happiness,
We who are nothing, we who spend a few years of nothing on earth,

A few wretched, pathetic years,
(We immortal souls),
O danger, the risk of death, it is we who are responsible,
We who are incapable of anything, who are nothing, who are uncertain
    of tomorrow,
And even of today, who are born and who will die like creatures of a
    day,
Who pass through like mercenaries,
And yet it is we who are responsible,
We who in the morning are uncertain of the evening,
And even of the afternoon,
And who at night are uncertain of the morning,
Of the following morning,
It's folly, it's still we who are responsible, it depends on us and us alone
To assure the Words a second eternity
An eternal eternity.
A remarkable perpetuity.
It belongs to us, it depends on us to assure the words
An eternal perpetuity, a carnal perpetuity,
A perpetuity nourished with meat, with fat and with blood.

We who are nothing, who will not last,
Who practically speaking won't last at all
(On earth)
It's folly, it's still we who are responsible to preserve and to nourish the
    eternal
On earth
The spoken words, the word of God.

Mystery, danger, happiness, misfortune, grace from God, special choice,
terrible responsibility, misery, glory of our life,
we ephemeral creatures, that is, who don't spend but a day,
who don't last but a day,
poor vagrant women who work like mercenaries,
who remain in a country merely to harvest the wheat or the grapes,
who work for a wage only for fifteen days or three weeks,
and who hit the road immediately afterward,
along the path,

turning the corner at the poplars,
we simple travelers, poor travelers, fragile travelers,
precarious travelers,
eternal vagabonds,
who enter this life and who immediately exit,
as vagabonds would enter a farm only for a meal,
for a crust of bread and for a glass of wine,
we feeble, we fragile, we precarious, we shameful, we weak creatures,
we flimsy, we transient creatures, we vagrants, we shepherds,
(but not, not at all strangers),
singular grace, (risk of what disgrace?),
Fragile creatures, it depends on us whether the eternal word
Resounds or does not resound.

In these carnal hearts, this, my child, is what the angels do not
        understand,
Other than by hearsay,
But they themselves have never experienced it,
In these carnal hearts, in these precarious hearts, in these vagrant hearts,
In these hearts that break
A word is preserved, is nourished
Which will never, for all eternity, break.

A word that will remain forever in these fragile hearts.

It's for this, my child, just for this,
(Are you still with me, you haven't lost your place),
It's for this that France, that Christianity must go on;
So that the eternal word doesn't fall into dead silence,
Into a carnal void.

Thus it's just for this,
(We're coming back, my child, you'll recognize the path),
It's precisely for this,
It's just for this, it's only for this,
That none of this,
And even nothing at all,
(So it is in this, by this, through this),

That absolutely nothing at all
Holds except because of the young child
Hope,
Because of she who continually begins again and who always promises,
Who guarantees everything.
Who assures tomorrow to today and this evening and this afternoon to
       this morning.
And life to life and even eternity to time.

Because of she who assures, she who promises to the morning, the day
   In its entirety,
To the spring, the year
   In its entirety,
To childhood, life
   In its entirety,
To time, eternity
   In its entirety,
To creation, God himself
   In his entirety.

To the harvest, wheat
   In its entirety,
To the vine, wine
   In its entirety.
To the kingdom, the king and to the king, the kingdom and so forth
       through the world over, and the eternal and the temporal, and
       the spiritual and the carnal,
And creation and God
Are held (with ease) in her tiny hands.

To assure this carnal perpetuity God must
(Miracle, the vase breaks
It even breaks perpetually,
And it doesn't lose a single drop of its liqueur[41]),
So that the word doesn't fall inert,
Like a dead bird, God must
Create these perishable creatures one after the other,
These men and these women,

(Who will become sinners and saints),
These parishes, one after the other, and in these parishes
(Miracle of miracles that the imperishable is only saved from perishing
        by the perishable)
(And the eternal is not nourished, is not maintained eternal except by
        the temporal)
And in these parishes, once founded, once created,
(Lorraine must, Toul must, Vaucouleurs must, Domrémy must go on),
In these parishes these perishable creatures, one after the other,
These (immortal) perishable souls, one after the other,
And these perishable bodies and these hearts,
In order to keep the imperishable word alive.

God must create them, one after the other, he must create them. They
        have to be born.
That's his business, it's his job, and we can be sure it is well done.
He provides for it, he provides for it eternally.
But what is our business, alas, and our job,
We perishable creations, perishable creatures,
Once created, once born, once baptized,
Once we are women and Christians,
What unfortunately depends on us, fortunately,
One after the other, is to nourish the living word,
To nourish for a time the eternal word.
After so many others, before so many others.
Ever since it was uttered.
Until the threshold of Judgment Day.

In saecula saeculorum.
Through centuries of centuries.
From generation to generation.
From the beginning of the centuries.
Until the consummation of the centuries
On earth.

As at the entrance of the church on Sunday and on the feast days,
When we go to Mass,
Or at the funerals,

        THE PORTAL OF THE MYSTERY OF HOPE

We give each other, we pass each other the holy water from hand to
    hand,
From neighbor to neighbor, one after the other,
Directly from hand to hand or from a blessed branch dipped into the
    holy water.
In order to make the sign of the cross either over ourselves, who are
    alive, or over the casket of the person who has died,
In such a way that the same sign of the cross is as if carried from
    neighbor to neighbor by the same water,
By the ministry, by the administering of the same water,
One after the other, over the same breasts and over the same hearts,
And the same foreheads too,
And even over the caskets of the same deceased bodies,
So from hand to hand, from finger to finger
From fingertip to fingertip, the eternal generations,
Who are eternally going to Mass,
In the same breasts, in the same hearts up to the death of the world,
Like a relay,
In the same hope, the word of God is passed on.

By the ministry, by the administering of the same hope.
By she who assures, by she who promises, by she who contains in
    advance.
By she who promises to eternity
    A time.
To the spirit
    A flesh.
To Jesus
    A Church.
To God himself
    A creation, (his creation, the creation),
Reversal, strange reversal, insane reversal,
By she who promises to the eternal
    A temporal.
To the spiritual
    A carnal.
To the Food
    A food.

To Life
    A life.
Reversal, it's as if
she were to promise
to life, a childhood,
to the year, a spring,
to the day, a morning.

As the faithful pass the holy water from hand to hand,
So we faithful, we must pass the word of God from heart to heart.
From hand to hand, from heart to heart, we must pass the divine
Hope.

It is not enough that we have been created, that we were born, that we
        were brought into the faithful.
We must, it depends on us as women and as faithful,
It depends on us Christians
To make it so that the eternal lacks nothing of the temporal,
(Strange reversal),
That the spiritual lacks nothing of the carnal,
It must be said, it's incredible: that eternity lacks nothing of time,
Of all time, of any particular time,
That the spirit lacks nothing of the flesh.
That the soul so to speak lacks nothing of the body.
That Jesus lacks nothing of the Church,
Of his Church.
We must go all the way: That God lacks nothing of his creation.

In other words it depends on us
To make it so that hope does not deceive the world.
That's to say, it must be said, it depends on us
To make it so that the greater does not lack the lesser,
That the infinitely greater does not lack the infinitely lesser,
That the infinitely everything does not lack the infinitely nothing.

It depends on us to make it so that the infinite does not lack the finite.
That the perfect does not lack the imperfect.

It's a wager, we are needed, it depends on us
To make it so that the great does not lack the small,
That the whole does not lack the part,
That the infinitely great does not lack the infinitely small.
That the eternal does not lack the perishable.

We are needed, (it's ridiculous), we are needed so that the Creator
Does not lack his creature.

And as on the last day there will be a great sign of the cross over the
    world's coffin.
Because it will be the final burial.
So on the last day there will be a great sign of the cross as a blessing.
Because it will be the fulfillment,
The crowning of hope.

Special grace, that a weakling, a weak creature carries God.
And that God could be in need of this creature.
It could be missing from his count and from his census,
When he counts his sheep, missing from his love and from his very
    being,
Making his hope to be a liar.

Because there is the crowning of thorns but there is also the crowning
    of hope.

Which is the crowning with branches from a tree without thorns.

Jesus Christ, my child, did not come to tell us tales.
During the little time that he had.
What is three years in the life of a world.
In the eternity of this world.
He didn't have any time to waste, he didn't waste his time telling us
    tales and playing charades for us to figure out.
Very witty charades.
Very clever.
A wizard's riddles.

Full of double-entendres and tricks and stupid subtleties and
     complexities.
No, he didn't waste his time and he didn't take pains,[42]
He didn't have the time,
His pains, his great, his very great pain.
He didn't waste, he didn't expend all of that, all of his being, everything.
He didn't spend himself, spend everything, he didn't make this
     enormous, this terrible expense
Of self, of his being, (of) everything,
To come afterwards, with this, by means of this, at this price,
To come at this price to give us some code to decipher
To decode.
Tricks, silly nonsense, quid pro quos, clever little antics like a
     fortuneteller from the town.
Like a village clown.
Like a traveling acrobat, a charlatan in his cart.
Like the town prankster, like the funniest guy in the tavern.

But when the Son of God, my child, took his leave of heaven and of
     his post at the right hand of his Father.
When he took his leave from his seat at the right.
He did not do it, he did not furnish this great expense,
He did not go through all this trouble to come talk nonsense
Worthless nonsense.
Idle words.
And senseless stories.
Rather, at this price, he came to tell us what he had to tell us.
Didn't he.
Calmly.
Simply, honestly.
Directly. Right from the start.
Ordinarily.
Like one honest man speaks to another honest man.
Man to man.
He didn't play around and twist everything up.
He had something to tell us, he told us what he had to tell us.
He didn't tell us something else.
And he didn't tell us anything that he didn't have to tell us.

THE PORTAL OF THE MYSTERY OF HOPE

What he had to say, he spoke.
Imbeciles are the ones who try to be clever.
Who try to see something where it's not.[43]
Now, when your mother sends you to run an errand at the bakery.[44]
When you go to the bakery,
You don't all of a sudden start recounting extraordinary stories to the
        baker.
You do what you were sent to do and you come back.
You take your bread, you pay, and you leave.
For him it's the same thing, he came to run an errand for us.
He had an errand to run for us on behalf of his father.
He did for us what he was sent to do and he went back.
He came, he paid (what a price!), and he left.
He didn't come recount for us extraordinary stories.
Nothing is simpler than the word of God.
He told us things that were quite ordinary.
Very ordinary.
The incarnation, salvation, redemption, the word of God.
Three or four mysteries.
Prayer, the seven sacraments.
Nothing is as simple as God's glory.
He spoke to us without digressions or complications.
He didn't put on airs, embellish things.
He spoke uniformly, like a simple man, crudely, like a man from town.
A man from the village.
Like a man in the street who doesn't search for his words and doesn't
        make a fuss.
When he chats.
Also, given that he spoke to us and that he spoke to us directly,
Given that he spoke to us in parables,
Which we call similitudes in Latin,
Since he didn't come to tell us tales,
Since he always spoke to us directly and plainly
To the letter,
On the level,
Always in response, we must always hear him and listen to him literally.
Directly and fully on the level.

Our brother, our big Brother did not trick us for the pleasure of being
    clever.
We ought not to trick him for the pleasure of playing the fool.
And it would be tricking him to look for mischief where he didn't put
    it.
To hear, to search, to want to hear; to imagine;
To warp;
To hear his word other than how he said it.
Even to listen other than how he spoke.

It's even the greatest deception that we could do to him.

To receive him another way, contrary to how he gave himself.

It's the greatest insult, it is perhaps the only insult we could give him.

A crown was made once: it was a crown of thorns.
And his face and his head were bloodied under this crown of derision.
And the blood beaded up in drops and the blood thickened in his hair.

But another crown was also made, a mysterious crown.
A crown, an eternal crowning.
All made, my child, all made of supple branches without thorns.
Budding branches, branches from the end of March.
April branches and May branches.
Flexible branches which braid easily into a crown.
Without a single thorn.
Very obedient, well guided by the hand.
A crown was formed from buds and shoots.
From flower buds like on a beautiful apple tree, from the buds of
    leaves, from the buds of limbs.
From the buds of branches.
From flower buds for flowers and for the fruit.
Fully budding, fully sprouting, a crown was made.
A mysterious crown.
All eternal, all set in advance, all swollen with sap.
All scented, all fresh to the world, all soft and fragrant.
All set for today, for before, for tomorrow.

THE PORTAL OF THE MYSTERY OF HOPE

For eternally,[45] for the day after tomorrow.
All made of tiny little shoots, of soft shoots, of the beginnings of
     shoots.
Leafy shoots, blossoming early,
Which are the shoots of soft, fresh buds,
And which have the smell and which have the taste of leaves and of
     flowers.
The taste of growth, the taste of earth.
The taste of tree.
And beforehand the taste of fruit.
Autumn fruit.
To soothe his poor forehead thrashed with fever, burdened with fever
In order to recover, to repay the crowning of derision,
To soften, to appease, to soothe, in order to refresh his throbbing
     temples,
His feverish temples.
His burning forehead, his feverish forehead,
Heavy with fever, his hot temples, the ache and the shame, and the
     headache and to soothe the derision itself.
To appease, to embalm, to slake the blood that thickened in his hair.
A crown has also been made, a crown of sap, an eternal crown,
And that's the crown, the crowning of hope.

As a mother makes a diadem with her outstretched fingers, her fingers
     from her two cool hands joined and intertwined
Around her child's burning forehead
To soothe his burning forehead, his fever,
So an eternal crown was braided to soothe his burning forehead.
And it was a crown of greenery.
A crown of foliage.

You must have confidence in God my child.
You must have hope in God.
You must trust God.
You must give God a chance.

You must have this confidence in God in order to have hope in him.
You must trust God in order to have hope in him.

You must give God a chance in order to have hope in him.

You must extend hope to God.

You must hope in God, you must have faith in God, it's all one, it's all
the same thing.
You must have this faith in God in order to hope in him.
You must believe in him, which is hoping.

You must have confidence in God, he certainly has had confidence in
us.
You must trust God, he certainly has put his trust in us.
You must hope in God, he has certainly hoped in us.
You must give God a chance, he has certainly given us a chance.
What chance.
Every chance.
You must have faith in God, he certainly has faith in us.

Remarkable mystery, the most mysterious,
God made the first move.
Or rather it's not a distinct mystery, it's not a particular mystery, it's a
mystery which bears on all the mysteries.
It's an increase, it's a growth to infinity of all the mysteries.
It's a miracle. A perpetual miracle, a miracle in advance, God made the
first move, a mystery of all the mysteries, God took the
initiative.
Miracle of all mysteries, remarkable mysterious overturning of all the
mysteries.
All of the feelings, all of the movements that we ought to have for God,
God had them before us, he began by having them before we did.
Remarkable overturning that runs through all the mysteries,
And makes them grow, increases them to infinity,
You must have confidence in God, my child, he certainly has had
confidence in us.
He had enough confidence in us to give us, to entrust us with his only
son.
(Alas alas what we did with him.)
The overturning of everything, it's God who took the initiative.

THE PORTAL OF THE MYSTERY OF HOPE

It's God who gave us a chance, who put his trust in us.
Who gave us credence, who had faith in us.
Will this confidence be misplaced, will it be said that this confidence
     was misplaced.

God put his hope in us. He took the initiative. He hoped that the least
     of the sinners,
That the tiniest of the sinners would at least work a little for his own
     salvation,
Just a little, as poorly as it might be.
That he would look after it a bit.
He hoped in us, will it be said that we didn't hope in him.
God placed his hope, his poor hope in each one of us, in the tiniest of
     the sinners. Will it be said that we tiny ones, that we sinners,
     will it be we who do not place our hope in him.

God entrusted us with his son, alas, alas, God entrusted us with our
     salvation, to take care of our salvation. He made his Son and
     our salvation and thus his hope itself depend on us; and we
     won't put our hope in him.

Mystery of mysteries, bearing on all the mysteries themselves,
He put his eternal hope in our hands, in our weak hands,
In our ephemeral hands.
In our sinful hands.
And we, we sinners, we won't put our weak hope
In his eternal hands.

The word of God is not a tangled ball of yarn.
It's a beautiful woolen thread which winds itself around the spindle.
As he spoke to us, thus we ought to listen.
As he spoke to Moses.
As he spoke to us through Jesus.
As he spoke to us all, thus we ought to listen.

Yes, my child, if that's how it is, if it's like this that we ought to listen
     to Jesus.
That we ought to listen to God.

Literally.
To the letter.
Strictly, simply, plainly, exactly, soundly.
On the level.
Then my child what a trembling, what a commandment of hope.
What an opening up, what a shock of hope. What a crushing. The
    words are there.
There's nothing to analyze, what an entry into the thoughts of God.
Into the will of God.
Into the intentions, (the ultimate intentions), of God.
Abyss of hope, what an opening, what lightning, what thunder, what a
    passageway.
What an entrance.
Irrevocable words, what an entry into the very Hope of God.
God deigned to hope in us. Hope for us.
Revelation, what an incredible revelation. *Sic non est, Thus it is not.*
Incredible hope, unhoped-for hope *Thus it is not*
Voluntas ante Patrem vestrum, the will before your Father,
Qui in caelis est, Who is in heaven.
Ut **unus**. That **a single one**
Of these little ones. De pusillis istis.
Pereat. Should perish.[46]

And he told them this parable, saying:
Which one of you, if he had a hundred sheep;
(This is according to St. Luke);
And if he lost one of them,
Would not dismiss, (would not leave), *the ninety-nine in the desert,*
And look for the one,

quae perierat, *which* **was** *lost, which* **had** *perished,*

That's what had happened.

Until he finds it?
And when he finds it,
He places it on his shoulders rejoicing;

(He puts it) on his shoulders.

And returning to the house, he summons, (he calls), *his friends and*
  relatives, saying to them:

Rejoice, (be happy), *with me, because I found my sheep that had perished?*

I tell you,
There will be as much joy in heaven
Over one repentant sinner,
Than over ninety-nine righteous ones who have no need of repentance.[47]

Now what is repentance, my child, what is there thus in repentance.
    What is this secret virtue of repentance.
My child it's remarkable, it's strange, it's disturbing.
What is so extraordinary about repentance.
How disturbing it is.
What is this virtue, this secret, what must there be that is so
    extraordinary,
In repentance,
  so that this sinner,
So that one is worth a hundred, or, ninety-nine anyway,
(To be exact),
So that this sinner is worth so much,
So that this sinner, this single repentant sinner is worth as much,
    gladdens, causes as much joy in heaven as ninety-nine
    righteous ones who have no need of repentance.
And so that this lost sheep causes so much joy for the shepherd,
For the good shepherd,
That he would leave in the desert, *in deserto,* in a forsaken place,
The ninety-nine sheep that were not lost.
In what, what then is this mystery,
What does this one have that makes him worth ninety-nine.
Aren't we all God's children. Equally and on the same footing.
In what, how, why would one sheep be worth ninety-nine sheep.
And especially why is it precisely the one that was lost, *that had*
    perished, that's worth precisely the ninety-nine others, the
    ninety-nine that were not lost.

Why, what is this mystery, what is this secret, it's suspicious, how, why, in what would one soul be worth ninety-nine others, it's a bit much.

In any case it's a bit much, when you think about it.

What is this intrigue.

It's precisely the soul that was lost, that had perished, that's worth as much, that causes as much joy in heaven as these ninety-nine others.

As these ninety-nine that were not lost.

Ever.

That did not stray, that had not perished.

Ever.

That had remained firm.

It's unfair. What is this invention, this new invention.

It's unfair. Here is one soul, (and it's precisely the one that was lost), who is worth as much, who counts as much, who causes as much joy as these poor ninety-nine others that had remained constant.

Why; in what; how. Here is one who weighs as much in God's scales as ninety-nine.

Who weighs as much? Who perhaps weighs more. In secret. You never know. It worries me. Secretly you have the impression that it weighs more, when you read the parable.

So here's a sinner, let's say, who weighs at least as much as ninety-nine righteous ones.

Who perhaps even weighs more. You never know. Once you've entered the sphere of injustice.

You never know where you'll end up.

Let's use the word unbeliever, you have to admit it, there's no reason to be afraid of the word.

Here is an unbeliever who's worth more than a hundred, more than ninety-nine believers.

What is this mystery.

What is this extraordinary virtue of repentance.

That surpasses a hundred times faithfulness itself.

We don't have to explain it to ourselves. We know very well what repentance is.

A penitent is someone who isn't very proud of himself.

THE PORTAL OF THE MYSTERY OF HOPE

Who isn't very proud of what he's done.
Because what he did, we must admit it, is a sin.
A penitent is someone who is ashamed of himself and of his sin.
Of what he did.
Who would like very much to hide himself.
Who above all wishes that he hadn't done it.
    Ever.
Hide himself, shield himself from the face of God.
And what, too, is this silver coin that's worth nine others, all by itself.
How does it figure into this.
And it's this one, and no other, it's this sheep, it's this sinner, it's this
        penitent, it's this soul
That God, that Jesus carries on his shoulders, abandoning the others.
That is, I mean (just) leaving them alone during this time.
Repentance, we know, is not really as glorious as that.
It doesn't glow quite that much.
(It is true that God never leaves anyone.)
It's a shameful feeling, I mean it's a feeling of shame.
Of a legitimate and due shame.
In short it's a shamefaced act.
Repentance isn't really quite as brilliant as all that. But so what.
Not only is this penitent worth another, not only is he worth as much
        as a righteous one, which would already be a bit bold.
But he's worth ninety-nine of them, he's worth a hundred of them, he's
        worth the whole herd.
We may as well say it.
With this feeling you have that he's worth more and that he's loved
        more.
    In the secret of your heart.
    In the secret of the eternal heart. So what.
My child, my child, you know what. It's precisely because.

He was lost; and has been found.
He was dead; and now he lives again.
He was dead; and now he is risen.

Because you have to take everything word for word, my child.
Literally, as Jesus was dead and is risen from the dead,

So this sheep was lost, so this sheep was dead,
So this soul was dead and from his own death he is risen from the dead.

He caused the very heart of God to tremble
With the shudder of worry and with the shudder of hope.
With the shudder of anxiety.
A mortal anxiety.
And so, and thus, and also
With that which is tied to worry, to fear, to anxiety.
With that which follows worry, fear, anxiety.
With that which walks alongside them, with that which is tied to
          worry, to fear, to anxiety
With an indelible bond, with an unbreakable bond,
With a temporal, eternal, and unbreakable tie
He caused God's heart to tremble
With the very shudder of hope.
He introduced into God's heart the theological virtue of
Hope.

Therein, my child, lies the secret. Therein lies the mystery.
Right there is the (hidden) glory, right there is the incredible source of
          glory that exists in this repentance.
In this shameful repentance. Secretly, publicly shameful and truly
Perhaps the most glorious of all. Is that a man's repentance
Should be the crowning of God's hope.

This shameful repentance, ashamed of itself, and which doesn't know
          where to hide itself.
Where to hide its face, ashamed, its face red with shame, purple with
          shame,
Its head covered with ashes and dirt,
As a sign of shame and of penitence,
Where to hide its shame and its sin.
But God is not ashamed of it.
Because the wait for this repentance,
The anxious waiting, the hope for this repentance
Triggered hope into God's heart,
Incited a new feeling,

THE PORTAL OF THE MYSTERY OF HOPE

Practically unknown, as if it were unknown, I know what I mean to say,
Caused a feeling, as if it were unknown, to rise, to beat in the very
      heart of God.
As though it were a new heart.
As if it were a new God. I understand, I know what it is I'm saying.
Of an eternally new God.

And this very repentance
Was for him, in him, the crowning of hope.

As for the others, God loves them in love.
But Jesus also loved this sheep in hope.
And all the others, God loves all of us in charity.
But the sinner, there once was a time when God loved him in hope.

You have to take everything word for word, my child. God hoped,
      God waited for him.
God, who is everything, had something else to hope for, from him,
      from this sinner. From this nothing. From us. He was put in
      this position, he put himself in this position, in the situation
      of having something to hope for, to await something from this
      miserable sinner.
Such is the strength of the life of hope, my child,
The strength of life, the promise, the strength of the life and the
      promise that springs from the heart of hope.
And that resurges in repentance itself,
In lowly repentance.

Such is the remarkable strength of the sap in the heart of an oak.

We are all God's children, my child, equally; on the same footing.

We must listen to everything word for word, my child, this soul, who
      literally triggered hope in God, was the crowning of God's
      hope.
This soul who was dead, like Jesus (more dead than Jesus), by its own
      death, is risen from the dead.

(More dead than Jesus, infinitely more dead, eternally more dead,
    because it had died the eternal death.)
Like Jesus it is risen from the dead.
And as we vigorously ring our Easter bells to celebrate the resurrection
    of Jesus,
Christus is risen! [48]
So God, for each soul that is saved, rings the *eternal* Easter bells.

And he says: I told you so.

Strange reversal, strange overturning, it's the world upside-down.
The virtue of hope.
All the feelings that we ought to have for God,
God already began by having them for us.
It's he who put himself in this position, in this situation, who was
        placed here, who allowed himself to be placed here, in this
        position, in this situation, to begin by having them for us.
Remarkable virtue of hope, strange mystery, she's not a virtue like the
        others, she is a virtue against the others.
She takes the counterposition of all the other virtues. She stands, as it
        were, against the others, against all the others.
And she stands up to them. To all the virtues. To all the mysteries.
She backs them up, so to speak, she goes against the current.
She fights the current of the others.
She's not at all a slave, no, this child is hardheaded.
She talks back, as it were, to her sisters; to all the virtues, to all the
        mysteries.
When they go down she goes up, (she's the one who's right),
When all go down she alone goes up, and thus she doubles them, she
        increases them tenfold, she increases them to infinity.

It's she who causes this reversal, this overturning that's stronger than
        any,
(It's perhaps the greatest thing she does),
(Who would have believed that such power, that supreme power had
        been given to this little child
Hope)
This overturning in which everything that we're supposed to do for God

THE PORTAL OF THE MYSTERY OF HOPE

God has already made the first move, God has begun by doing it for us.
Everything that we're supposed to tell him, do for him, do unto him.
And all that we're supposed to have for God,
God has begun by having for us.

He who loves places himself, by loving,
By that very act, from then on, into dependence,
He who loves becomes the slave of the one who is loved.
It's normal, it's the common lot.
It's inevitable.
He who loves falls into slavery, consigns himself, puts himself under
      the yoke of slavery.
He becomes dependent on the one he loves.
And yet it's this very situation, my child, that God made for himself, in
      loving us.
God has deigned to hope in us, because he wanted to hope for us, wait
      for us.
Miserable situation, (in) return for what love,
Pledge, ransom of what love.
Strange reward. And which was within the conditions, within the order
      itself, within the nature of this love.
He put himself in this strange, reversed situation, in this miserable
      situation where it's he who waits for us, for the most miserable
      sinner.
Who *hopes* for the most miserable sinner.
And us.
This is where he allowed himself to be led, by his great love, this is
      where he was put, where he put himself, or in any event,
      where he allowed himself to be put.
This is where it's got him, where he is.
Where we should be, that's where he put himself.
In this position, in this situation.
That he has to worry, to hope, finally to wait for the least of men.
That he is in the hands of the least of the sinners.
(But the body of Jesus, in the whole of the Church, isn't it in the
      hands of the least of the sinners.
At the mercy of the least of the soldiers.)[49]
That he has everything to fear from us.

(That he should have anything to fear, that's already too much, that's
        already everything),
(That he should have the least bit to fear, and here it's everything)
(As little as it might be, even if it's hardly anything, even if it's nothing,
        so to speak)
Such is the situation in which God, by the virtue of hope
In order to wager hope,
Allowed himself to be placed
Before the sinner.
He stands in fear of him, because he fears for him.
You see what it is I'm saying: God stands in fear of the sinner, because
        he fears for the sinner.
When you fear for someone, you stand in fear of that person.
God allowed himself to be placed under this universal law.
To be submitted.
To this common level.
God suffered to be placed under this universal law.
He has to wait for the sinner's own sweet time.
He put himself in this situation.
He has to hope in the sinner, in us.
He has to, it's insane, he has to hope that *we* save *ourselves*.
He can't do anything without us.
He has to listen to our excuses.
He has to wait for Mr. Sinner to get around to thinking about his own
        salvation.

That is the situation that God made for himself.
He who loves becomes the slave of the one who is loved.
Just by loving.
He who loves becomes the slave of the one he loves.
God did not desire to evade this universal law.
And by this love he becomes the slave of the sinner.

The overturning of creation, it's creation upside-down.
The Creator now depends on his creature.
He who is everything placed himself, suffered to be placed, allowed
        himself to be placed on this level.

He who can do everything depends on, waits for, hopes for the one
   who can do nothing,
(And who can do everything, alas, because everything has been given
   over to him,
Everything has been entrusted to him,
Everything has been granted to him,
Everything has been given over to him, into his hands, into his sinful
   hands,
In confidence,
In hope,
He has been permitted everything.
In all confidence.
He has been given over, he has been permitted to care for his own
   salvation, the body of Jesus, the hope of God.)
God put himself in this situation. As the most miserable creature was
   freely able
To slap freely the face of Jesus,
So the least of creatures is able to make God to be a liar
Or to make him speak truly.
Terrible delegation of power.
Terrible privilege, terrible responsibility.
As Jesus through centuries of centuries has given over his body
In the poor churches
To the discretion of the least of the soldiers.
So God through centuries of centuries has given over his hope
To the discretion of the least of the sinners.
As the victim surrenders his hands to the executioner,
   So Jesus has abandoned himself to us.
As the prisoner abandons himself to the prison guard,
   So God has abandoned himself to us.
As the least of the sinners was able to slap Jesus,
   And it had to be so,
So the least of the sinners, a miserable, weak creature,
The tiniest of sinners is able to bring to failure, is able to bring to
   fulfillment
   A hope of God;
The tiniest of sinners is able to uncrown, is able to crown
   A hope of God.

And it's from us that God awaits
   The crowning or the uncrowning of one of his hopes.

Terrible love, terrible charity,
Terrible hope, truly terrible responsibility,
The Creator has need of his creature, put himself in need of his
         creature.
And can't do anything without it.
A king who has abdicated into the hands of each one of his subjects
Merely absolute power.
God *needs* us, God *needs* his creature.
He has, as it were, condemned himself thus, condemned himself to this.
He lacks us, he lacks his creature.
He who is everything needs him who is nothing.
He who can do everything needs him who can do nothing.
He has handed over his full power.
He who is everything is nothing without him who is nothing.
He who can do everything can do nothing without him who can do
         nothing.

Thus the young hope
Takes over, takes up, remakes,
Straightens out all the mysteries
Just as she straightens out all the virtues.

We are capable of failing him.
Not responding to his call.
Not responding to his hope. Being absent. Missing it.
   Not being there.
Terrible power.
God's calculations are capable of turning out wrong because of us.
God's plans, forethoughts, providences.
Are capable of turning out wrong because of us.
Through the fault of the sinful man.
God's counsels are capable of turning out lacking because of us.
God's wisdom is capable of failing because of us.
Man's terrible freedom.
We could make a mess of everything.

We could be absent.
Not be there the day we're called.
We could fail to respond to the call
(Except in the valley of Judgment)
Terrible favor.
We could fail God.
These are the circumstances in which God has placed himself.
The bad circumstances.
He put himself in the circumstances of needing us.
What rashness. What confidence.
Well or misplaced confidence, that all depends on us.
What hope, what obstinacy, what one-sidedness, what incurable
        strength of hope.
In us.
What a divestment, of self, of power.
What rashness.
What lack of planning, what lack of foresight, what lack of providence
        for God.
We could be absent.
We could go wrong.

We could be failures.
Terrible favor, terrible grace.
He who does everything appeals to him who can't do anything.
He who does everything needs him who does nothing.
And as we ring out our Easter bells,
At full volume,
In our poor, in our triumphant churches,
In the sun and beautiful weather of Easter day,
So God, for each soul that saves itself
Rings out the eternal Easter bells.
And says: Hey, I was right all along.
I was right to have confidence in this boy here.
He was good-natured. He came from good stock.
Son of a good mother. He was a Frenchman.
I was right to trust him.
And we have our beautiful Sundays,
Our beautiful Sunday, Easter Sunday,

And Easter Monday,
And even Easter Tuesday, which is also a feast day,
Because the feast is so big,
(It's the feast of St. Loup[50]).
But God also has his Sundays in heaven.
His Easter Sunday.
And he also has his bells, when he wants them.

And what, too, is all this about the ten silver coins.
Which is like saying ten Parisian pounds.
What is this yet about this business of ten silver coins.
What has this one coin done that makes it worth nine others.
Strange calculation, like saying one Parisian pound is worth nine others,
Nine others of the same thing. What strange arithmetic.
And yet this, my child, is how the books are kept with God.

This, my child, is how the books were kept with Jesus.
    It's undeniable; there's no doubt that there are two families of saints in
        heaven.
Two types of saints.
(Fortunately they get along well together.)
Just as the king's soldiers and his captains
Are from one line or another, and yet are all Frenchmen.
And, all the same, they form a single army.
And they are all the king's soldiers (in his army), and his captains.
But it's just that they come from one province or another.
From one region. Some from one, others from another.
Or from beyond the Loire or, around here, from the Loire.
Thus, (and for other reasons), you have to say, you have to admit that
        there are two families of saints in heaven.
Two temporal families.
Two types of saints.
Everyone is a sinner. All men are sinners.
    But ultimately there are two great families, there are two sources of
        recruits.

There are two recruitments of saints in heaven.

THE PORTAL OF THE MYSTERY OF HOPE

There are those who come from, there are those who emerge from the
        ranks of the righteous.
And there are those who emerge from the ranks of the sinners.
And it's a difficult enterprise.
It's an undertaking that's impossible for man.
To know who are the greatest saints.
They're so great on both sides.

There are two extractions (and yet all, together, equally, are saints in
        heaven. On the same footing) (God's saints)
There are two extractions, those who come from the righteous and
        those who come from the sinners.
Those who have never caused any serious anxiety
And those who have caused
A (mortal) anxiety.
Those who have not triggered hope and those who have triggered hope.
Those who never caused any worry, any serious dread, and those who
        have almost caused despair, God preserve us.
Those whom we've never heard anything about.
And those about whom we've heard uttered
The (mortal) word.

There are two formations, there are two extractions, there are two
        families of saints in heaven.
God's saints come out of two different schools.
The school of the righteous and the school of the sinner.
The wavering school of sin.
Fortunately in both cases God is the schoolmaster.

There are those who come from the righteous and those who come
        from the sinners.
And it's obvious who is who.
Fortunately there's absolutely no jealousy in heaven.
   On the contrary.
Because there is the communion of saints.
Fortunately no one there is jealous of anyone else. But all together, on
        the contrary, they are as close as fingers on the hand.

Because all of them all together spend all the time of their holy day
      plotting together against God.
In God's presence.
So that Justice, step by step,
Gives way, inch by inch, to Mercy.

They do violence to God. Like good soldiers they fight every inch of
      the way,
(They wage war against justice.
They're forced to)
To save the falling souls.
They hold out. All moved, all inspired by hope,
Boldly against God,
(But they also receive support, a patronage, divine protection.
What a patron, my children, and what a patroness.)
What (other) plot above theirs, encompassing their great plot,
Lending patronage to their great plot.
What an advocate next to God.
(Advocata nostra).[51]
Because our patrons and our saints, our patrons the saints
Themselves have a patron and a patroness.
A man and a woman saint.
Who are as far
(And seventy times farther) above them as they are above us
Themselves.
Who are for them what they are for us, and seventy times what they
      are for us.
Such is the folly of hope.
And encompassed, encouraged by this divine plot,
By the protection of this divine plot,
All nourished by hope they hold out like good soldiers.
They fight step by step, they defend their territory step by step
We can't even imagine everything they do, everything they come up
      with
To save these falling souls.
Bit by bit, they snatch up
A soul in danger
From the kingdom of Hell.

THE PORTAL OF THE MYSTERY OF HOPE

Thus God did not want,
It wouldn't have pleased him,
To have only one voice in the concert.
It would not have been pleasing to his wisdom.
Nor to his liking.
He did not wish to be praised with a single voice.
By a single choir
Nor fought.
But, as in a country church there are several voices
That praise God.
For example the men and the women.
Or even the men and the children.
So in heaven it pleased him, it was pleasing to his wisdom.
And it was to his liking.
To be praised, to be sung, to be fought by two voices.
By two languages, by two choirs.
By the former righteous ones and by the former sinners.
So that, step by step, Justice would draw back
   Before Mercy.
And that Mercy would advance.
   And that Mercy would pull ahead.
Because if there were only Justice and if Mercy were not to get involved,
Who would be saved.

Or what woman having ten silver coins,
(It is again according to St. Luke, my child),
If she lost one coin,
If she lost one of them,
Would she not light a lamp,
And sweep the house,
And search carefully,
Until she found it?

And when she does find it,
She summons her friends and her neighbors,
(They always summon their friends and their neighbors in these
       parables),
Saying:

Rejoice with me,
Because I found the coin that I had lost.

Thus I tell you,
There will be joy among the angels of God,
Over one repentant sinner.[52]

There was a grand procession; at the head of the procession went the
      three Similitudes;
  the parable of the lost sheep;
  the parable of the lost coin;
  the parable of the lost child.[53]

Now just as a child is more precious than a sheep,
And infinitely more precious than a coin,
Just as a child is dearer to his father's heart,
(His father who is at the same time, who is already, who is first, who is
      primarily his shepherd),
Dearer even than a sheep is to the heart of the (good) shepherd,
By just so much the third Similitude,
By just so much the parable of the lost child
  Is more beautiful, if possible, and more precious,
Is greater than the two preceding Similitudes,
Than the parable of the lost sheep,
And than the parable of the lost coin.

All of the parables are beautiful, my child, all the parables are great, all
      the parables are precious.
All the parables are the word and the Logos,
The word of God, the word of Jesus.
They are all equally, they are all together
The word of God, the word of Jesus.
On equal footing.
(God placed himself in this situation, my child,
In the unfortunate situation,
Of needing us)
They all come from the heart, equally, and they go to the heart,
They speak to the heart.

              THE PORTAL OF THE MYSTERY OF HOPE

But among them all the three parables of hope
Advance,
And among them all they are great and faithful, among them all they
       are reverent and affectionate, among them all they are
       beautiful, among them all they are dear and close to the heart.
Among them all they are close to man's heart, among them all they are
       dear to man's heart.
They have, in a sense, a special place.
They have something in them that's not, that isn't in the others.
It's perhaps that they have in them a certain youth, a certain childhood.
Unknown and unsuspected elsewhere.
Among them all they are young, among them all they are fresh, among
       them all they are children, among them all they are unspoiled.
Unaged.
Not spoiled, not aged.
Throughout the thirteen and fourteen centuries that they've served, and
       throughout two thousand years and through centuries of
       centuries, they have been as young as on the first day.[54]
Fresh, innocent, naive,
Children as on the first day.
And for the thirteen hundred years that there have been Christians and
       for fourteen hundred years,
These three parables, (may God forgive us),
Have held a special place in the heart.
And may God forgive us as long as there will be Christians,
As long, that is, eternally,
Through the centuries of centuries there will be, for these three
       parables,
A special place in the heart.

And all three of them are parables of hope.
Together.
Equally young, equally dear.
Among them.
All three sisters like three very young children.
Equally dear, equally special.
Specially loved. Equally loved.
And as if more personal than all the others.

As if answering to a deeper inner voice.
But among them all; among the three of them the third parable
     advances.
And this one, my child, this third parable of hope,
Not only is it new as on the first day.
Like the two others
Her sisters.
And not only will it be new through centuries of centuries,
Just as new until the last day.
But for the fourteen hundred, for the two thousand years that it has
     served,
And that it has been told to innumerable men,
(From the first time it was told),
To innumerable Christians,
Unless one had a heart of stone, my child, who could hear it without
     crying.

For fourteen hundred, for two thousand years it has made innumerable
     men cry.
Through the centuries and through the centuries.
Innumerable Christians.
It has touched a unique place in man's heart, a secret place, a
     mysterious place.
(It reaches the heart.)
A place that's inaccessible to the others.
There may not even exist a place that's more inward and more
     profound.
Innumerable men, from its first telling, innumerable Christians have
     cried over it.
(Unless they had a heart of stone.)
Have cried because of it.
Through the centuries men will cry.
Just by thinking about it, just by seeing it, who could,
Who would be capable of holding back their tears.
Through the centuries, through eternity men will cry over it; because
     of it,
Whether they be believers or unbelievers.
Through eternity, until judgment day.

Up to the judgment itself, through the judgment. And
It's the word of Jesus that has carried the farthest, my child.
It's the one that's had the greatest luck.
Temporal luck. Eternal luck.
It has awakened in the heart a certain point of resonance
A special resonance.
It has also been especially fortunate.
It's famous even among the impious.
It has found, even with them, a point of entry.
Alone perhaps it has remained driven into the heart of the impious
Like a nail of tenderness.
Then he said: A man had two sons:[55]
And he who hears it for the hundredth time,
It's as if it were the first time.
That he heard it.
A man had two sons. It is beautiful in Luke. It is beautiful everywhere.
It's not only in Luke, it's everywhere.
It's beautiful on earth and in heaven. It's beautiful everywhere.
Just by thinking about it, a sob rises in your throat.
It's the word of Jesus that has had the greatest effect
On the world.
That has found the deepest resonance
In the world and in man.
In the heart of man.

In the believing heart, in the unbelieving heart.

What sensitive spot has it found
That none had found before it,
That none had found, (to the same extent), since.
What a unique point,
Unsuspected before,
Unobtained ever since.
A point of suffering, a point of distress, a point of hope.
A sore spot, a spot of anxiety.
A tender spot in man's heart.
A spot that one shouldn't press, a place of scarring, a place of laceration
        and of scarring.

That one shouldn't press.

Special point, special fortune, special strength of attachment.
Special bond, special link between the believing heart.
And the unbelieving heart.
All of the parables are beautiful, my child, all the parables are great.
And especially the three parables of hope.
And all three of the parables of hope, moreover, are young, my child.
But hundreds and thousands of men have cried over this one.
Hundreds and thousands of men.
Because of this one.
Choked by the same sobs, cried the same tears.
Believers and unbelievers.
Beginning all over again, one after the other.
The same way.
Wracked by the same sobs.
In a communion of tears.
Laid out, doubled over, raised up from the same sobs, cried the same
    tears.
Believers and unbelievers.
Shaken by the same sobs.
Crying like children.

A man had two sons. Of all of God's parables
This one has awakened the deepest echo.
The most ancient echo.
The oldest, the newest echo.
The freshest echo.
Believer or unbeliever.
Known or unknown.
A unique point of resonance.
The only one that the sinner has never been able to silence in his heart.
Once this word of hope has bitten into his heart
Into his believing or unbelieving heart,
No pleasure will ever more be able to erase
Its teeth-marks.[56]
Such is this word. She's a word that stays with you.[57]
She follows like a dog

That remains even though you beat it.
Like a mistreated dog, who always comes back.
She remains faithfully, she comes back like a faithful dog.
There's no use kicking her or beating her with a stick.
She's faithful
With a special fidelity,
She thus accompanies man into his greatest
Follies.
She is the one who teaches that all is not lost.
It is not God's will
That a single one of these little ones should perish.
She's a faithful dog
Who bites and who licks
And by both sustains
The inconstant heart.
When the sinner turns away from God, my child,
As he turns away, as he buries himself in lost countries, as he loses
       himself.
He tosses along the way his most precious goods,
Among the stones and bramble, as things useless and heavy and which
       hinder him. His most sacred possessions.
The word of God, his purest treasures.
But there is one word of God that he does not throw away.
Over which every man has cried so many times.
Over which, because of which. By which.
And he's like the others, he too has cried.
There is one of God's treasures, when the sinner turns away
To the growing darkness,
When the shadows
The lengthening shadows
Veil his eyes, there is one of God's treasures that he will not toss among
       the bramble at the side of the road.
Because she's a mystery that follows, she's a word that follows
Into the most extreme
Estrangements.
There's no need to look after her, and to carry her.
    It's she.

Who looks after you and who carries herself and who makes sure she is
    carried.
It's she who follows, she's a word that stays with you, a treasure that
    accompanies.
The other words of God don't dare accompany man
Into his greatest
Follies.
But in truth she is shameless.
She holds man by the heart, at a point that only she knows, and does
    not let him go.
She's not afraid. She's not ashamed.
And as far as man might stray, this man who loses himself,
In whatever country,
In whatever darkness,
Far from the hearth, far from the heart,
And whatever shadows he may have buried himself in,
The shadows that veil his eyes,
A spark will always keep watch, a flame will always keep watch, a
    tongue of flame.
Always a light that will keep watch and that will never be placed under
    a bushel basket. Always a lamp.
Always a simmering pang. *A man had two sons.* A pang he knows well.
A source of anxiety within false contentedness, a source of hope. All
    the other words of God are modest. They don't dare
    accompany man into the shamefulness of sin.
They aren't forward enough.
Into his heart, into the shamefulness of his heart.[58]
But she in truth is not shameful.
You could say that she is rather adventurous.
She's a little sister of charity who's not afraid to handle a sick person or
    a poor person.
She has, as it were,
And even truly, delivered a challenge to the sinner.
She has told him: Wherever you go, I'll follow.
You'll see.
With me you will have no peace.
I will not leave you in peace.
And it's true, and he knows it. And ultimately he loves his persecutor.

THE PORTAL OF THE MYSTERY OF HOPE

In the depths of his heart, secretly.
Because at the very bottom of his heart, at the bottom of his shame
and of his sin he loves (better) not having peace. It's kind of
reassuring.

A point of suffering remains, a point of thought, a point of anxiety. A
bud of hope.
One light will not go out and it's
the third Parable,
the third word of hope. *A man had two sons.*

There was a great procession. At the head of the procession, the three
Similitudes
moved ahead. Faith, says God, is not very tricky.
Everyone believes. I'd really like to see how they could do otherwise.
Yes I'd like to know what they could do not to believe.
How they'd go about it.
I'm so resplendent in my creation.
Even in the depths of the sea and in its salty abyss.
In the depths of the abyss.
In the thunder and lightning of a stormy sky,
When the sky is heavily charged.
The lightning that rips apart the sky.
In zigzags.
In the roar of the thunder that rips apart the sky.
And in the rolling of a distant thunder.
In the rolling and the unrolling of thunder.
And in those beautiful days when there isn't the slightest breeze
In May.

Short of blindness, what could they do not to see me.
Love, says God, is not very tricky. It doesn't surprise me either.
These poor children are so unhappy that unless they had a heart of
stone
How could they not love their brothers.
How could they not love each other.

But hope, says God, *(a man had two sons),* that these poor children see
      how things go every day.
And every day they believe that things will go better the following
      morning.
Precisely the following morning.
Every day since there have been days.
And that a better sun will rise.
And when they wake up every morning they believe it will be a great
      day.
Today.
And when they go to bed every night they believe that tomorrow.
That precisely tomorrow, that the very following day
Will be, will make a good day.
For all the time that there have been days.
And that it will start all over again.
That all the disappointments don't count, all those disappointments
      that they receive precisely every day.
That the disappointments are nothing, don't stop them, that the
      disappointments of every day,
As innumerable as the days,
Innumerable in the innumerable days, that the disappointments
Do not disenchant them of this idea, of this absurd conviction
That today's day will be a better day,
Another day, a new day, a fresh day, a brand-new day,
A day that rises,
Freshly washed,
A day, in short, a good full day.
In short,
A day not like the others,
After so many others which were, every one of them, like the others,
That he's even forgotten.
Forgotten as soon as they were over.
Forgotten as soon as they were lived.
Forgotten as soon as they were had.
That they believe that this morning, well, it'll be fine.
That things will go well.
That they believe even so, that this morning, things'll go well,
This is what confounds me.

This is what is beyond me.
And I myself can't get over it.
My grace must, indeed, be great.[59]

And that they instantaneously forget the bad days.
As they pass. Immediately.
Almost before. Almost in advance.
That they stifle, as it were, the memory of their bad days almost before
    they happen.
That they absorb the bad days almost before they've occurred.
Before they've gone by.
Before they've fallen through.
Before they've drawn to a close.
Like a fervent soil that absorbs the ingratitudes of heaven.
That they drink up the bad days, as it were, faster than the bad days
    fall.
More quickly.
The bad days that fall like an autumn rain.
Like a gray rainfall, like a tireless rain,
A merciless rain,
Falling, descending from a crisscrossed sky.
More so than from a gray sky.
Like a slanting, persistent rain.
That they take in everything that falls to them like the good soil of
    Lorraine,
Like a generous and healthy soil,
Like a fit, mild, and loose soil
  drinks up everything that falls and does not allow itself to be overrun
    by swamps and marshes.
And by pools and by shoals and by swamps full of mud and sludge,
And of the soul's dregs and of sticky
And slimy plants.
And slithery and slimy insects.
But, rather, from everything that falls and from the countless rains and
    from the countless bad days
Immediately, instantaneously, almost before the days fall they create a
    current of water.
Flowing water, clear water, sweet water.

Beautiful, translucent water.
Pure water that gushes and that flows in the meadows
On the banks of the Meuse.
Beautiful water from Lorraine, a soul of beautiful water and the spring
    itself of hope.[60]
That it should be precisely with this material, with these countless bad
    days that fall like rain
That they create, that they gush, that they produce, that they cause the
    very spring of hope to burst forth.
This unfathomable spring and this unfathomable river.
This river which is the greatest of all my rivers.
The only great one.
This is what I myself admire. And I know a lot about things.
I know my creation. And the work of the Six Days.
And the rest of the Seventh.
This is what surprises me. And yet I'm not easy to surprise.
I'm so old. I've seen so much. I've done so much.
This is what is beyond me and I myself can't get over it.
My grace must, indeed, be great.

The bad days fall; unhurriedly; tirelessly; hour after hour, day after day.
    The bad days fall.
And with all this water that trickles tirelessly from heaven, (the heaven
    that they could speak badly of),
With all this water that trickles to the earth, with all this slanting rain,
    (Others would have made it into marshes and swamps full of fever and
    overpopulated with dirty, disgusting insects).
But they, the good soil, my loose and well-cultivated soil.
My well-developed soil.
My good soil of souls, well plowed by my Son for centuries of centuries.
My good healthy soil of Lorraine, they take in this water that falls.
And, wonderfully, they do not make it into swamps and mud and
    sludge.
And algae and hart's-tongue and other bizarre plants.
But, wonderfully, it's this very water that they collect and which does
    not hinder them in the least.
Because, wonderfully, it's from this very water that they create the
    spring.

It's this water, it's the same water that runs along the meadows.
It's the same healthy water that flows in the stalks of wheat for the
    Bread.
It's the same healthy water that flows in the vines for the Wine.
It's the same healthy water that flows in both buds, in both shoots.
In both Laws.
It's the same collected water, it's the same water, healthy, purified, that
    flows around the world.
That returns, that reappears, having flowed around my whole creation.
It's the same collected water that bursts forth, that springs forth.
From the new fountain, from the young wellspring.
From the spring and resurgence of hope.

Truly, says God, my Son made me some very good gardeners.
For the fourteen centuries that he has loosened this soil of souls.
For the fourteen centuries that my Son has tilled and cultivated this
    soil,
He made me some very good plowmen and cultivators.
And harvesters and vine-growers. Fine vine-growers.
These bad days that fall like rain and that everywhere else would
    poison entire countries.
Entire nations, entire populations, entire creations.
This rain upon rain which everywhere else would overrun,
Would engulf the vegetable soil with a grimy silt,
Would drown every shoot and bud
With the ruin and the worms of sludge.
All these bad days that fall like rain
Would everywhere else flood, would drown, with stains, with smudges,
The good vegetable soil,
Would bog down, would cover with plagues
The whole of my creation,
But here, says God, in this gentle France, my most noble creation,
In this healthy Lorraine,
Here they are good gardeners.
Here, there are old, accomplished gardeners, expert gardeners from the
    fourteen centuries that they've followed my Son's lessons.
They have channelled everything, loosened everything in the gardens of
    the soul.

The water that would have flooded, would have poisoned *(laughing)*
    they use instead to irrigate.
My Son's people, a people full of grace, eternally full of youth and of
    grace.
The very waters of heaven you divert; for your marvelous gardens.
My anger itself you divert; for your mysterious, for your marvelous
    gardens.
The plagues themselves you divert and they don't strike you and you
    use them only as fertilizer
For your mysterious, for your marvelous gardens.
O people you have learned my Son's lessons well.
My Son who was a great Gardener.
My specially loved people, you have turned out the best.
My gardening people, a healthy water shall forever irrigate your soils.
People; people who do not retreat before any pestilence.
O my French people, o my people of Lorraine. Pure people, healthy
    people, gardening people.
People of plowmen and cultivators.
People who plow the soil and souls.
The deepest.
Your water shall forever be living water.
And your springs, gushing fountains.
Your streams shall forever be rivers and running waters.
And your hidden springs in your mysterious.
In your marvelous, in your sorrowful gardens.
Shall forever be a running water, a healthy water shall irrigate your
    fields.
A healthy water shall forever flow in your Wheat.
A healthy, rare, abundant water, a precious water, a healthy water shall
    forever flow in your Vines.
People who make the Bread, people who make the Wine.
O my soil of Lorraine, o my French soil,
People who have best followed, who have best taken in my Son's
    lessons.
People who work with the little child Hope.
Who springs up everywhere in this land.
And in the mysterious.
In the marvelous, in the very sorrowful gardens of souls

        THE PORTAL OF THE MYSTERY OF HOPE

Gardening people who have raised the most beautiful flowers
Of sanctity
By the grace of the little Hope.

People who repel pestilence
With order. With cleanliness, with integrity; with clarity.
With a virtue you have in you, with a true virtue, with a special virtue.
Gardening people, who till and who harrow,
Who spade and who rake,
Who loosen creation itself.
And I say, says God, I proclaim: Nothing is deeper than a plowed field.
And nothing is as beautiful, I know these things.
Nothing in my creation is as great
As the beautiful gardens of well-ordered souls, like those of the French.
All the wild beauty of the world, if you want my opinion; surely, I
        know something about it,
All the wild beauty of the world is not worth a garden in the French
        style.
Because it's there that you'll have the most soul and the most creation.
It's there that you'll have soul.
Mysterious gardens, marvelous gardens,
Sorrowful gardens of French souls.
All the wild beauty of the world is not worth one beautiful French
        garden.
Honest, modest, and in order.
That's where I gather my most beautiful souls.
All the wild beauty of the world is not worth one beautiful
        organization.
Honest people, people of gardeners, you have grown the most beautiful
        souls
Of sanctity.
Sorrowful gardens of souls have grown there
Which have suffered without disrupting the arrangement
The most difficult martyrdom
Without destroying the order.[61]
And I know how much that costs.
Sorrowful gardens where souls have grown that I have gathered
In their sorrow.

All the wild beauty of the world is not worth one presbytery's garden.
With its turnsoles.
That the children call suns.
And they are suns, if I want them to be.
A good garden of the country priest.
Peaceful; quiet.
Where I've gathered my most beautiful souls.
My silent souls.
Savages will say that this garden is not great and that it is not profound.
But I know, (says God), that nothing is as great as order and that
    nothing is as deep as tilling.
The way the French do it.
Honest people, full of youth,
Full of my youth and of my grace.
The waters of heaven do not intimidate you.
You are not hindered by them, the waters of heaven you divert.
The bad days rain and rain, and they do not corrupt you.
On the contrary, o people who purify everything.
France, my eldest daughter.
You don't see the bad days as corruption and pestilence.
As corrupt water, as stale water.
You do not make of the bad days stagnant waters.
Foul and slimy.
But as gardeners, as a gardening people you make them into beautiful
    brooks of living water.
Which irrigate the most beautiful gardens
That have ever existed in the world.
Which irrigate the gardens of my grace, my eternal gardens.
I know, says God, how far a Frenchman can hold his tongue
Without disrupting the arrangement.
I know to what lengths a Frenchman can go so as to keep from
    destroying order.
And how they suffer inwardly, and to what extent,
What trials they bear, without moving from the line,
Like a beautiful bridge, like a beautiful, sturdy archway.
What sacrifices they bring to me, (in secret), no sacrifice is as deep
As the tilling of the French.
A pure water, a healthy water, flowing water rises

In the stalks of the law of the Bread.
A healthy water, a rare water, flowing water rises
In the vines of the law of the Wine.
Water from Lorraine, French water rises in the budding
Of both laws.
You French, says God, have invented these beautiful gardens of souls.
I know what marvelous flowers grow in your mysterious gardens.
I know what trials
You bear tirelessly.
I know what flowers and what fruits you bring to me in secret.
You are the ones who have invented the garden.
The others create only horrors.
You are the ones who design the King's garden.
And I tell you in truth, you are the ones who will also be my gardeners
        before God.
You will design my gardens of Paradise.

There must be something going on, says God, between our French and
        the little Hope.
They work so wonderfully together.

Industrious people, people of the deepest tilling.
They are not a people who stagnate and wallow in the swamps of sloth.
In the stagnant bogs, in the cesspools, in the dead marshes.
In the stagnation and in the mud of sloth.
In the stagnation of despair.
In the stagnation and in the mud of sin.
Alert people, gardening people, with whom the bad days
Do not settle, the bad days do not seep
Into stagnant bogs, but these people of the market-gardens
Make the swamps themselves into the most beautiful gardens.
They grow the finest vegetables, the finest fruits.
Their soul is always flowing water and living water.
And their work is always flowing water.
And their prayer, I know, is always flowing water.

Remarkable people, there must be, says God, some special relationship.
Some special intimacy.

There must be some sort of relationship between this people and the
    little Hope.
They work too well together.
And they're the only ones who work well together.
There must be between them some sort of adoption.
They have adopted hope and hope has adopted them.
Not, of course, like a father adopts a daughter and a daughter adopts a
    father.
But more intimately.
An intimacy, a more intimate adoption.
They're with her, (I understand the families of men), like an uncle with
    his niece.
When an uncle lives with the family, he has with the children
And likewise the children have with him
A certain freedom, their own intimacy
That the father will never have.[62]
A certain complicity, a secret understanding that's never mentioned.
But they don't have any reason to mention it.
They don't need to mention it even to themselves.
In order to see it.
It's just there.
The father is the immediate authority figure, he's got the earnest brow,
    the frowning eyes, he's burdened with the direct responsibility.
And the children feel it.
He's above them.
And the children feel it.
The bond between the father and the son is a sacred bond, that has
    weight, it's a direct line.
And the children feel it.
The uncle has a certain freedom, (and at the same time, age and
    experience), he does whatever he wishes, he is for the children
All the fun of life.
The children know it. With him and him alone, from him the remarks
    are funny, from him with him and him alone the games are
    fun.
He alone has this intimacy.
It's like this that the two of them are joined up, the French and the
    little Hope.

THE PORTAL OF THE MYSTERY OF HOPE

She only enjoys herself with them.
She listens to all their conversation. There is none but theirs.
Everything they say is great. She's grateful toward them.
Only their stories are interesting. She never leaves their lap. She makes
them retell the stories twenty times over.
This is the sort of relationship the French have with the little girl Hope.

Remarkable people, for them, all water is a living spring.
For them, all water that falls from heaven becomes flowing water.
By the ministering of hope.
For them, all water, all bad water becomes drinkable.
The bad water often makes them sick.
But the bad water never poisons them.
They drink everything with impunity.
Because of the relationship they have with the little girl Hope.

You may wonder, you may ask yourself: But how is it
That this fountain of Hope flows eternally,
That it gushes eternally, that it springs eternally
That it flows eternally,
Eternally young, eternally pure.
Eternally fresh, eternally flowing.
Eternally living.
Where does this child get so much pure water and so much clear water.
So much gushing, so much surging.
Does she create it? As she needs it?
— No, says God, I am the only one who creates.
— So where does she get all this water.
For this gushing fountain.
How is it that this eternal fountain
Gushes eternally.
That this eternal spring
Springs eternally.
There must be a secret there somewhere.
Some sort of mystery.
For this spring to remain eternally untroubled by the thick, by the
heavy autumn rains.

For it eternally to keep from running dry during the blazing heat of
    July.
    — My good people, says God, it's not tricky.
Her mystery is not tricky.
And her secret is not complicated.
If she wanted to make pure springs out of pure water,
If she wanted to make springs of pure water,
Then she'd never find enough of it, in (the whole of) my creation.
Because there's not a whole lot of it.
But it's precisely with the impure water that she makes her springs of
    pure water.
And that is the reason she never runs out.

But that's also why she is Hope.

Now how does she go about making pure water from impure water,
Young water from old water,

Young days from old days.
New water from used water.

Springs from old water.
Fresh souls from old souls.

Fountains of soul from old soul.
Cold water from lukewarm water.

Woe to he who is lukewarm.[63]

Young mornings from old evenings.
Clear souls from troubled souls.

Clear water from troubled water.
Childlike water, childlike souls from used souls.

Rising souls from setting souls.
Flowing souls from stagnant souls.

How does she accomplish this, how does she go about it,
That, my children, is my secret.
Because I am her Father.

New souls from souls that have outlived their service.
New days from days that have outlived their service.

Limpid souls with troubled souls.
Rising souls with setting souls.
Limpid days with troubled days.

If it were from limpid days that she made limpid days.
If it were with souls, with clear water that she made her springs.
From clear water that she made clear water.
If it were from pure souls that she made pure souls,
Heavens, that would be nothing. Anyone could do as much. And there
    wouldn't be any secret to it.

But it's from sullied water, old water, stale water.
But it's from an impure soul that she makes a pure soul and that's the
    most beautiful secret in the whole garden of the world.

If it were from pure water that she made pure water, she knows what
    she's up to, she's tricky.
If it were from pure water, if it were from pure water that she produced
    a spring of pure water,
She'd run out of it immediately.
She's not so stupid, she knows that she'd run out of it immediately.

But it's from impure water that she makes an eternal spring.
    She knows well that she'll never run out of it.
The eternal spring of my grace itself.
    She knows well that she'll never run out of it.
My grace must, indeed, be great.
It's from impure water that she makes her fountains.
    She'll never run out of this, either.
Her perfectly pure fountains.
It's from the impure day that she makes the pure day.

She'll never run out.
It's from the impure soul that she makes the pure soul.
She'll never run out.

There was a grand procession. It was the procession for Corpus Christi.
They carried the Holy Sacrament. And at the head, the three
Theological Virtues
Were marching. Look, says God, how the little one marches.
Just take a look.
The others, the two others, her older sisters, march like grown-ups.
They know who they are. They're well dressed. They know
that they're in a procession.
Especially in a procession for Corpus Christi.
Where the Holy Sacrament is displayed.
They know what a procession is.
And that they're in the procession, at the head of the procession.
They move along with the procession. They hold themselves well. They
march ahead like grown-ups.
Like serious grown-ups. Who are always a little tired.
But she's never tired. Take a look at her.
Look at how she marches.
She's twenty steps ahead of them, like a little puppy, she comes back,
she leaves again, she makes the trip twenty times.
She has fun with the garlands in the procession.
She plays with the flowers and the leaves
As if they weren't sacred garlands.
She plays by jumping on top of the foliage
The freshly cut, freshly gathered foliage that's strewn about.
She doesn't listen to anything. She doesn't stay in place during the
stations.
She'd rather keep marching. Keep moving ahead.
Keep jumping. Keep dancing. She's so happy.
(O people, gardening people, who grow the roses of France
For the processions.
The king's gardeners, gardeners of flowers and fruits, gardeners of souls,
O people, you are my gardeners.
Gardeners in the orchard, gardeners in the vegetable patch, gardeners in
the garden.

Even gardeners in the field.
Gardening people, honest people, clean people.
People with integrity.
Your forests are cleaner than the king's park itself.
Your woods [your wildest woods] are cleaner than the king's orchard.
Your fields and valleys are cleaner than the king's garden.
I don't find a single weed in your most expansive fields.
Industrious people I look in vain, your fields are as pure as a beautiful
    garden.
And your valleys that slope gently in the distance.
Are full of fertility. Bursting with fruits. With their secret hollows.
Diligent people, the plow and the harrow and the roller, the spade and
    the rake and the pickaxe and the hoe and the biddle and the
    line
Never grow bored in your hands.
Are never idle in your hands.
You're not afraid to touch them. You don't look at them solemnly from
    a distance.
But the plow and the harrow and the roller and the shovel and the
    pickaxe and the spade and the hoe.
You make honest workers out of them, tools of an honest man.
You're not afraid of approaching them.
The palm of your hand polishes the handle of the tool, and gives it the
    beautiful shine of wood.
The handle of the tool polishes the palm of your hand, and gives it the
    beautiful shine of leather.
A yellow shine.
You make your tools into agile tools. Diligent tools. Honest tools.
Tools that move quickly. And that've got a good handle on them.
First people, you are the first in the vegetable patch.
The first in the orchard. The first in the garden.
The first in the field.
You are alone in all of this.
You raise the finest vegetables and the finest fruits.
You gather the finest vegetables, you gather the finest fruits.
You even gather the finest leaves.
You scatter the finest foliage
At the feet of the three Theological Virtues.

At the grave feet of my daughter Faith, you lay the most beautiful, the
    most serious foliage
That is strewn or scattered.
At the bleeding feet of my ardent daughter, of my daughter Charity,
    you lay the most beautiful, the gentlest foliage
That is strewn or scattered.
The coolest to her feet.
Foliage so cold that its freshness rises straight to her heart and even to
Her dry lips. Cool foliage
That's like a balm for the suffering heart.
Since it's like a balm for suffering feet
For bleeding feet, for bloodstained feet. At the feet of Cinderella, of my
    little child Hope.
People, you toss the most ebullient foliage
That is strewn or scattered. Foliage filling the streets. And scattered at
    the feet of the great Processions.
People, at the feet of the great Holy Sacrament,
At the feet of the Very Great one; people, you sow the roses of France.
People, you lay at the feet of the great Processions
The greatest Flowers, the greatest Leaves.
The most beautiful, the greatest flowers on this carnal earth.
The greatest flowers in the world.
The terrestrial world.
The greatest flowers of earth and of soul.
The greatest flowers of bloodline and of soil.
Nourished with water.
And with soil.
People, you have made a garden of your realm.
The king's garden. The king's realm.
People, you have made a garden of your fields.
People, who, without reckoning, at the feet of the Most High,
Scatter flowers, scatter souls,
Knowing that there will always be flowers and souls.
And that you will always make them grow.
People, people, the only ones who never reckon with me.
People of the king, kingly people, I say to you, I will take you to the
    king.
I, too, am king and I will take you to the king for my kingdom.

Gardeners of the king, I will take you to the king
On the day of the Crowning
So you can design my gardens
In my kingdom of Heaven.
People, I will make you my gardening people.
Friends of the line and of the biddle.
And you will make me the beautiful roses of France.
And the beautiful white lilies of France.
That wear the undrooping collar.

People of nurserymen, people of rose gardens, scrupulous people.
Patient people, who have the patience [and the taste] to weed.
People who are constantly weeding. Faster and more constant and
        more persevering than nature itself.
More bent over the soil, more bowed, more bent on weeding, you who
        move more quickly and are more constant and more
        persevering in weeding
Than the weed is in growing [and that's saying a lot]
Than spiteful nature itself is in growing the spiteful weed.[64]
People who are more sufficient in pulling up the spiteful weed than
        spiteful nature is in making it grow.
[And that's saying a lot. If anyone should know, it's me.]
People more stubborn, more patient, more persistent than spiteful
        nature itself,
When I look over your fields I look in vain, I don't see a weed.
Not a thistle for the asses. Not that darnel that my Son called tares
And that he often used for his similitudes. *A man had two sons.*[65]
And that you also call darnel or couch grass.
Industrious people, when I look over your fields.
Nor do I find that terrible disease in your harvests.
When the wheat *has the disease.* And especially the rye.
That ergot, that decaying of the rye, that terrible
Dry rot that poisons
That dares to poison the bread itself.

When I look over your fields, Frenchmen,
I wish you could thus rid
Your souls as well

Of all the weeds of sin.
Of the decay, the hateful disease that eats away at
The Eternal Bread.

People who throw by the armful
The beautiful lilies of France with the undrooping collar,
Scattered,
Strewn,
Freshly cut,
At the feet of the Most Holy and Immaculate one.)

Look at the little one, says God, how she marches.
She would skip rope in the procession.
She marches, she moves ahead by skipping a rope, for a bet.
She's so happy
(Alone among them all)
And she's so sure that she'll never get tired.
Children walk exactly like little puppies.
(Moreover, they play like puppies too)
When a puppy goes for a walk with his masters
He comes and he goes. He comes back, he leaves again. He goes ahead,
        he returns.
He makes the trip twenty times.
Covers twenty times the distance.
It's because as a matter of fact he's not going somewhere.
His masters are the ones who are going somewhere.
He's not going anywhere at all.
What he's interested in is precisely making the trip.
Likewise with children. When you make a trip with your children
When you run an errand
Or when you go to Mass or to Vespers with your children
Or to say the rosary
Or between Mass and Vespers when you take a walk with your children
They trot along in front of you like little puppies. They run ahead,
        they lag behind. They come and they go. They play around.
        They jump.
They make the trip twenty times.
It's because as a matter of fact they're not going somewhere.

THE PORTAL OF THE MYSTERY OF HOPE

They're not interested in going somewhere.
They're not going anywhere at all.
The grown-ups are the ones who are going somewhere
The grown-ups, Faith, Charity.
The parents are the ones who are going somewhere.
To Mass, to Vespers, to say the rosary.
To the river, to the forest.
To the fields, to the woods, to work.
Who do their best, who strain themselves in order to get somewhere
Or even to go somewhere to go for a walk.
But the children are only interested in making the trip.
To come and to go and to jump. To wear out the road with their legs.
Never to have enough of it. And to feel their legs growing.
They drink up the road. They thirst for the road. They never have
        enough of it.
They're stronger than the road. They're stronger than fatigue.
They never have enough of it (just like hope). They run faster than the
        road.
They don't go, they don't run in order to get there. They get there in
        order to run. They get there in order to go. Just like hope.
        They don't spare their steps. The idea doesn't even occur to
        them
To spare anything at all.
It's the grown-ups who are sparing.
Alas they're forced to be. But the child Hope
Never spares anything.
It's the parents who are sparing. Unhappy virtue, alas, that they should
        have to make a virtue of it.
They're forced to. As strong as my daughter Faith is,
Solid as a rock, she's forced to be sparing.
As ardent as my daughter Charity is,
Burning like a fine wood fire
That warms the poor man by the fireplace
The poor man and the child and the starving man,
She's forced to be sparing.
Only the child Hope
Is she alone who never spares anything.
She doesn't spare her steps, the little devil, she doesn't spare ours.

Just as she doesn't spare the flowers and the leaves in the grand
       Processions,
And the roses of France and the beautiful Lilies of France
With the undrooping collars,
So in the little, in the long procession, in the hard procession of life
       she doesn't spare anything
Neither her steps nor ours.
In the ordinary, in the gray, in the common procession
Of everyday
(Because it's not every day that you have Corpus Christi.)
She doesn't spare her steps, and since she treats us like herself
She doesn't spare ours either.
She doesn't spare herself; and likewise, she doesn't spare others either.
She makes us start the same thing over twenty times.
She makes us return twenty times to the same place.
Which is generally a place of disappointment
(Earthly disappointment.)
It doesn't matter to her. She's like a child. She is a child.
It doesn't matter to her to take the grown-ups for a ride.[66]
Earthly wisdom is none of her business.
She doesn't calculate like we do.
She calculates, or rather she doesn't calculate, she counts (without
       noticing) like a child.
Like someone who has her whole life in front of her.
It doesn't matter to her to take us for a ride.
She believes, she expects us to be like her.
She doesn't spare our sufferings. And our trials. She thinks
That we have our whole lives ahead of us.
How she deceives herself. How right she is
For don't we indeed have our whole Life ahead of us.
The only one that matters. Our whole Eternal life.
And doesn't the old man have as much life ahead of him as the baby in
       the crib.
If not more. Because for the baby in the crib the eternal Life,
The only one that matters, is hidden by this miserable life
That he has in front of him. First. It's in front. By this miserable life
       on earth.

THE PORTAL OF THE MYSTERY OF HOPE

He has to endure, he has to go through this whole miserable life on
    earth
Before he can get to, before he can reach, before he can attain the Life
Which is the only life that matters. The old man is lucky.
He has wisely left behind this miserable life
Which had hidden the eternal Life from him
And now he is free. He has put behind him what was before.
He sees clearly. He's full of life. There's no longer anything between
    him and life. He's standing on the edge of the light.
He's on the shore itself. He's at the limit. He's on the brink of eternal
    life.
We are right in saying that old men are wise.
Just as the child is right to think
That we are like her.
That we have our whole life ahead of us.
That we have it as much as she does. That it matters for her
To make us make the trip twenty times.
She's right. What matters
(And to make us return twenty times to the same place
Which is generally a place of disappointment
Of earthly disappointment) what matters
Is not to go here or there, is not to go someplace
To arrive someplace
Some earthly place. What matters is to go, always to go, and (on the
    contrary) not to arrive.
What matters is to go simply in the simple procession of ordinary days,
The great procession toward salvation. The days pass in procession
And we pass in procession through the days. What's important
Is the going. To keep going. That's what matters. And how you go.
It's the road you travel. It's the traveling itself.
    And how you do it.
You make twenty times the same trip on earth.
    To come to an end twenty times.
And twenty times you end up, you come to, you attain
With difficulty, with much effort, with much straining,
Painfully
The same point of disappointment.
Of earthly disappointment.

And you say: This little Hope has tricked me again.
I never should've trusted her. It's the twentieth time that she's tricked
      me.
(Earthly) wisdom is not her strong point.
I will never believe her again. (You will believe her again, you will
      always believe her).
I'll never get taken in again. — Fools that you are.
What does it matter the place you wanted to go to.
Where you thought you were going.
Come on now, you're not children, you know perfectly well
That the place you were going to would be a disappointment.
An earthly disappointment. It was already disappointing beforehand.
      So why did you want to go there.
Because you understand very well the game of this little Hope.
Why do you always follow this child of disappointment.
Why do you get yourself involved in this little one's game.
All the time, and the twentieth time more firstly than the first.
Why do you go along of your own accord.
All the time, and the twentieth time more readily than the first.
It's because in your heart you know very well what she is.
And what she does. And that she fools us.
Twenty times.
Because she is the only one who does not fool us.
And does not disappoint us
Twenty times
All through life
Because she is the only one who does not disappoint us
For Life.
And it's thus that she is the only one who does not disappoint us.
Because those twenty times that she makes us take the same trip
On earth, according to human wisdom, those are twenty times of
      increasing difficulty
Of repetition, of the same thing
Twenty times in vain, right on top of each other
Because they all went by the same road
To the same place, because it was the same route.
   But for God's wisdom
Nothing is ever nothing. All is new. All is other.

        THE PORTAL OF THE MYSTERY OF HOPE

All is different.

In God's sight nothing repeats itself.

Those twenty times that she made us take the same trip to get to the
same point

Of futility.

From the human perspective it's the same point, the same trip, the
same twenty times.

But that's the deception.

That's the false calculation and the false reckoning.

Being the human reckoning.

And this is why it doesn't disappoint: Those twenty times are not the
same. If those twenty times are twenty times of trial(s) and if
the route is a path to sanctity

Then along the same path the second time doubles the first

And the third time triples it and the twentieth time multiplies it
twenty-fold.

What does it matter to arrive here or there, and always at the same
place

Which is a place of (earthly) disappointment.

What matters is the path, and which path you take, and what you do
on it

How you take it.

It's the trip alone that matters.

If the path is a path to sanctity

In God's sight, a path of trials

He who takes it twice is twice as holy

In God's sight, and he who takes it three times

Is three times as holy, and he who takes it

Twenty times, twenty times more holy. That's how God reckons.

That's how God sees things.

The same path is not the same the second time around.

Every day, you say, all your days are alike

On earth, all days are the same.

Departing from the same mornings they convey you to the same
evenings.

But they do not lead you to the same eternal evenings.

Every day, you say, looks the same. — Yes, every earthly day.

But have no fear, my children, they do not at all look like

The last day, which is different from every other.
Every day, you say, repeats itself. — No, they are added
To the eternal treasury of days.
The bread of each day to that of the day before.
The suffering of each day
(Even though it repeats the suffering of the day before)
Is added to the eternal treasury of sorrows
The prayer of each day
(Even though it repeats the prayer of the day before)
Is added to the eternal treasury of prayers.
The merit of each day
(Even though it repeats the merit of the day before)
Is added to the eternal treasury of merits.
On earth everything repeats itself. In the same matter.
   But in heaven everything counts
And everything increases. The grace of each day
(Even though it repeats the grace of the day before)
Is added to the eternal treasury of graces. And it's for this that the
         young Hope
Alone doesn't spare anything. When Jesus worked at his father's shop[67]
Every day he relived the same day.
There was never any trouble
Except once.
And yet this is the fabric, within these days of sameness,
This is the web of the same workdays
That make up, that eternally make up
The admirable Life of Jesus before his preaching
His private life
His perfect life, his model life.
The life he offers as an example, as an inimitable Model to imitate
To everyone, without a single exception, only leaving to certain ones
To certain rare chosen ones (and still it's in addition and not to the
         contrary)
The examples of his public life to imitate
The inimitable models of his Preaching
And of his Passion and of his Death.
(And of his Resurrection.)
Similarly, together with him, in imitation of him

THE PORTAL OF THE MYSTERY OF HOPE

On earth, along our paths of earth our steps erase our steps.
Because the paths of earth are unable to preserve several layers of tracks
But the paths of heaven eternally preserve every layer of tracks
All of our footprints.
Lining the paths of earth there is only one material, earth,
Our earthly paths are always made from the same earth
And it's the same earth that's used every time, and it can be useful only
     one time
At a time.
It's the same earth that's used every time.
It only ever preserves one layer of tracks at a time.
In order to receive one it must sacrifice another.
The one before. Always the one before.
One track erases the other. One step erases the other step. One foot
     erases the other foot.
That's why we say that we're taking the same path.
The same path is the same path, the same path made from the same
     earth.
In the same earth.
But the paths of heaven eternally receive imprints.
New ones.
And he who walks at the eleventh hour down the paths of heaven *(A*
     man had two sons)[68]
To go to work and he who returns from work
Impresses a new imprint in the soil
   an eternal imprint
Which is his own imprint; and he eternally leaves
Intact the imprints of all those
Who came before him. Who have passed since the first hour.
And even and likewise
He leaves intact the very imprints of the one
Who had passed just before him.
It's the miracle itself of heaven, the everyday miracle of heaven, but on
     earth
He that follows erases the steps of the one who precedes.
Steps erase steps
In the same sand.
He who walks behind erases the steps of the one who walks ahead.

And we, too, when we take
When we repeat twenty times the same path
When, twenty times over, we walk behind ourselves,
We ourselves erase the tracks of our (own) steps.
Of our former steps.
And yet that's what Jesus did
For thirty years.
In imitation of him, it's still what Jesus, what God asks of us
Of those who haven't received special vocations
Public vocations.
And even of the others.
We who haven't received special vocations
Public vocations.
And even of the others.
We who haven't received special vocations
Extraordinary vocations,
Public vocations,
For our whole lives.
And even of those who have received special vocations
Extraordinary vocations
Public vocations
During their entire private lives, and even beyond, and even after
During the thirty years of their private lives, and for even longer
Because even in the public life all the days look the same.
Departing from the same mornings and being conveyed toward the
        same evenings.
Because in all of life there are terribly few days that don't look like all
        the others.
But all these days count. In Jesus' life itself, in his public life itself
During his preaching, how many days were any different from the
        others.
How much of his preaching was any different and how much of it was
        not, temporally, a repetition.
There was only one day of the Institution of the Supper. And one day
        of the Crucifixion. And one day of the Resurrection.
(And there will only be one day of Judgment.)
For the thirty and for the three years every other day looked the same.

But all these days count. Because on earth we erase our own tracks
     twenty times
And we tread twenty paths on top of each other.
But in heaven, they don't fall on top of each other. They are placed
     end-to-end. And they make a bridge
That brings us to the other side.
A single one would be too short. A single path. But twenty end-to-end
(Even though each of the twenty is the same as the others)
Are long enough. Thus when we say that hope deceives us.
And when at the same time secretly in our hearts we conspire with her
To help her deceive us,
In our hearts we know very well what all this means.
And that this secret complicity we have with her
To help her deceive us
Is that within us
Which is most pleasing to God.
Yes, she treats us like herself.
As she treats herself.
As if we were like her.
That is, as if we were indefatigable.
And she makes us return twenty times along this path.
Which isn't the same.
As if we were indefatigable.
Children don't even think about being tired.
They run like little puppies. They make the trip twenty times.
And, consequently, twenty times more than they needed to.
What does it matter to them. They know well that at night
(But they don't even think about it)
They will fall asleep
In their bed or even at the table
And that sleep is the end of everything.
This is their secret, this is the secret to being indefatigable.
Indefatigable as children.
Indefatigable like the child Hope.
And always to start over again in the morning.
Children can't walk, but they really know how to run.
The child doesn't even think, doesn't know that he'll sleep at night.
That he'll fall asleep at night. And yet it's this sleep

Always at hand, always available, always present,
Always underneath, in full reserve,
That of yesterday, and that of tomorrow, like good food for one's being,
Like a strengthening of being, like a reservoir of being,
That's inexhaustible. Always there.
That of this morning and that of this evening
That strengthens his legs.
The sleep from before, the sleep from after
It's this same bottomless sleep
As continuous as being itself
Which passes from night to night, from one night to the next, which
      continues from one night to the next
By passing over the days
Leaving the days as days, like so many holes.
It's in this same sleep that children bury their whole being
Which maintains, which creates for them every day new legs,
Their brand new legs.
And also that which is in their new legs: new souls.
Their new souls, their fresh souls.
Fresh in the morning, fresh at noon, fresh in the evening.
Fresh like the roses of France.
Their souls with the undrooping collars. This is the secret to being
      indefatigable.
Just sleep. Why don't people make use of it.
I've given this secret to everyone, says God. I haven't sold it.
He who sleeps well, lives well. He who sleeps, prays.[69]
  (He who works, prays too. But there's time for everything. Both for
    sleep and for work.
Work and sleep are like two brothers. And they get on very well
    together.
And sleep leads to work just like work leads to sleep.
He who works well sleeps well, he who sleeps well works well.)

There must be, says God, some relationship,
There must be something going on
Between the kingdom of France and this little Hope.
There's some secret there. They work too well together. And yet they
    tell me

          THE PORTAL OF THE MYSTERY OF HOPE

That there are men who don't sleep.
I don't like the man who doesn't sleep, says God.
Sleep is the friend of man.
Sleep is the friend of God.
Sleep may be my most beautiful creation.
And I too rested on the seventh day.
He whose heart is pure, sleeps. And he who sleeps has a pure heart.
This is the great secret to being as indefatigable as a child.
To have that strength in your legs that a child has.
Those new legs, those new souls
And to start over every morning, always new,
Like the young, like the new
Hope. Yes, they tell me that there are men
Who work well and who sleep poorly.
Who don't sleep. What a lack of confidence in me.
It's almost worse than if they worked poorly but slept well.
Than if they worked but didn't sleep, because sloth
Is no worse a sin than anxiety
In fact, it's even a less serious sin than anxiety
And than despair and than a lack of confidence in me.
I'm not talking, says God, about those men
Who don't work and who don't sleep.
Those men are sinners, it goes without saying. They get what they had
    coming to them. Great sinners. All they have to do is work.
I'm talking about those who work and who don't sleep.
I pity them. I'm talking about those who work, and who thus
In doing this are following my commandment, poor children.
And who, on the other hand, don't have the courage, don't have the
    confidence, don't sleep.
I pity them. I hold it against them. A bit. They don't trust me.
As a child lays innocently in his mother's arms, thus do they not lay.
Innocently in the arms of my Providence.
They have the courage to work. They don't have the courage to do
    nothing.
They possess the virtue of work. They don't possess the virtue of doing
    nothing.
Of relaxing. Of resting. Of sleeping.
Unhappy people, they don't know what's good.

They look after their affairs well during the day.
But they don't want to give them to me to look after during the night.
As if I weren't capable of looking after them for one night.
He who doesn't sleep is unfaithful to Hope.
And that's the greatest infidelity.
Because it's an infidelity to the greatest Faith.
Poor children, they manage their affairs wisely during the day.
But, come nightfall, they can't resolve
They can't resign themselves to entrust their affairs to my wisdom
They can't allow me to govern their affairs for the space of one night.
To take over the management and government of their affairs.
As if I weren't capable, I suppose, of looking after them a bit.
Of watching over them.
Of managing and governing and all the rest.
I manage plenty of other affairs, poor people, I govern creation, surely
        that's more difficult.
Maybe you could, without much loss, leave your affairs in my hands,
        wise men.
Surely I am as wise as you are.
Perhaps you could hand them over to me for the space of a night.
While you sleep
At least
And maybe tomorrow morning you won't find them too badly
        damaged.
Maybe tomorrow morning they won't be any worse off.
I'm probably still capable of guiding them a bit.
   I'm talking of those who work
And who in this follow my commandment.
And who don't sleep, and who in this
Reject all that's good in my creation,
Sleep, all that I have created good,
And who reject all the same my same commandment.
What ingratitude these poor children have toward me
To reject such a good,
Such a beautiful commandment.
These poor children are following human wisdom.
Human wisdom says Never put off till tomorrow
What you can do today.

       THE PORTAL OF THE MYSTERY OF HOPE

Whereas I tell you He who can put off till tomorrow
Is he who is most pleasing to God.
He who sleeps like a child
Is he, too, who sleeps like my precious Hope.
And I tell you Put off till tomorrow
Those concerns and those worries that are eating at you today
And that might devour you today.
Put off till tomorrow those sobs that choke you
When you see today's misery.
Those sobs that rise in you and strangle you.
Put off till tomorrow those tears that fill your eyes and cover your face.
That flood you. That fall down your cheeks. Those tears flowing from
      your eyes.
Because between today and tomorrow, I, God, may have passed by.
Human wisdom says: Cursed is he who puts off till tomorrow.
And I say Happy, happy is he who puts off till tomorrow.
Happy is he who puts off. Which means Happy is he who hopes. And
      who sleeps.
And I say on the contrary Cursed.
Cursed is he who lies awake and doesn't trust me. What a mistrusting
      of me. Cursed is he who lies awake.
   And who drags.
Cursed is he who drags through the evenings and through the nights.
Through the eve of evening and through the fall of night.
Like a snail's trail across these beautiful eves.
My creatures.
Like a slug's trail across these beautiful nightfalls.
My creatures, my creation.
The thick remembrances of daily cares.
The burning, the gnawing.
The dirty tracks of our cares, the bitterness and the anxieties.
The sorrows.
The trails of slugs. Upon the flowers of my night.
Truly I tell you that this offends
My precious Hope.
Who wouldn't want to entrust me with the supervision of his night.
As if I hadn't proven myself.

Who wouldn't want to entrust me with the supervision of one of his
      nights.
As if I were asking for more than one.
Who, having surrendered his affairs in poor condition when he went to
      bed,
Has not found them well when he woke up.
Because I may have paid him a visit.

Nights follow each other and are linked together and for the child,
      nights are continuous and form the very basis of his being.
He falls back on them. They are the very basis of his life.
They are his being itself. Night is the place, night is the being wherein
      the child bathes, wherein he is nourished, wherein he is
      created, wherein he is made.
Wherein he makes his being.
Wherein he recovers.
Night is the place, night is the being wherein he rests, wherein he
      retires, wherein he collects himself.
Wherein he comes home. And leaves again refreshed. Night is my most
      beautiful creation.
Now why doesn't man make use of it. They tell me that there are men
      who don't sleep at night.
Night is for children and for my young
Hope what it is in reality. Children are the ones who see and who
      know. My young hope is the one who sees and who knows.
      What being is.
What this being, night, is. It's the night that's continuous.
Children know very well. Children see very well.
And it's the days that are discontinuous. It's the days that pierce, that
      break the night
And not at all the nights that interrupt the day.
It's the day that makes noise for the night.
Otherwise it would be sleeping.
And the solitude, and the silence of the night is so beautiful and so
      great
That it envelops, that it surrounds, that it enshrouds the days
      themselves.
That it forms a majestic barrier against the restlessness of the days.

Children are right, my little Hope is right.
   All the nights
Meet together, join together like a beautiful circle, like a beautiful dance
Of nights that hold each other by the hand, while the meager days
Only form a procession of days that do not hold each other by the
         hand.
Children are right, my little Hope is right. All the nights
Meet together, join together above the borders of the days,
         hand-in-hand
Above the days, forming a chain and more than a chain,
A circle, a dance, the nights take each other by the hand
Above the day, from morning to evening
From the edge of morning to that of the evening, leaning over toward
         each other.
The one that descends from the preceding day leans backward
The one that rises from the following day
Leans forward
And the two join together, joining their hands,
Joining their silence and their shadow
And their reverence and their majestic solitude
Above the troublesome borders
Above the borders of the toilsome day
And all together, thus hand-in-hand,
They pass above the borders, above the wrists bound
To wrists, all of the nights, one after the other,
Together form night; and the days, one after the other,
Together do not form day. Because they're never anything but meager
         days
That don't take each other by the hand. Now, in the same way that life
On earth
On a grand scale (if I can put it that way) is nothing but a passage
         between two borders
An opening between the night before and the night after
A hole
Between the night of shadows and the night of light
Thus on a small scale each day is merely an opening.
A hole.
Not only between the night before and the night after.

Between two borders.
But as the children see it, as the children feel it, and my young Hope,
    as the children know it,
An opening in night, in the one and only,
In the one and only night
Wherein being draws its strength.
In the depths of the night.
Night is what is continuous, wherein being draws its strength, night
    forms one long continuous fabric,
A boundless continuous fabric, whereas days are only holes.
Open up only like holes.
That is, like those little holes in material that has eyelets.
In a woven material, in a stitched fabric.
Night, on the other hand, is my great black wall
Whereas the days only open up like windows
Onto a restless, onto a wavering,
And perhaps onto a false, light.
Whereas days only open up like windows.
Whereas days only open up like skylights.
For it must not be said that the chain of time
Is an endless chain
Where joint follows joint, where link follows link,
Where the days and nights follow each other equally in the same chain.
A white link, a black link, night coupled with day, day coupled with
    night.
Because they aren't at all equal, they don't at all have the same dignity
    in this chain.
Night is what is continuous. Night is the fabric
Of time, the reservoir of being
And day only opens upon it by wretched windows and back doors.
It's the day that divides and the day only opens within it
Like miserable windows
Of suffering. It's the day that fractures and the days are like islands in
    the sea.
Like broken islands that break the sea.
But the sea is continuous and it's the islands that are wrong.
Likewise it's the days that are wrong and broken; they break the night.
But no matter what they do, they themselves

THE PORTAL OF THE MYSTERY OF HOPE

Bathe in the night.

As the sea is the reservoir of water so night is the reservoir of being.

It's the time that I've reserved for myself. No matter what these feverish days may do

As in the open sea, in the middle of the night, they bathe in the fullness of night.

It's they that are scattered, it's they that are fragmented.

The days are the Sporades Islands and night is the open sea

Upon which St. Paul sailed

And the border that descends from night to day

Is always a rising border

A steep border, and the border that rises from the day toward the night

Is always a descending border. In the depths of night.

 O night, my finest invention, my most noble creation of all.

My most beautiful creature. Creature of the greatest Hope.

You give the most substance to Hope.

You are the instrument, you are the very substance and the dwelling-place of Hope.

And also, (and thus), you are ultimately the creature of the greatest Charity.

Because it's you who gently rock the whole of Creation

Into a restoring Sleep.

As one lays a child in his little bed,

As his mother lays him down and as his mother tucks him in

And kisses him (She's not afraid of waking him up.

He's sleeping so soundly.)

As his mother tucks him in and laughs and kisses his forehead

For pleasure.

And he too laughs, he laughs in response while sleeping.

So too, o night, dark-eyed mother, universal mother,

Not only mother of children (it's so easy)

But even mother of men and of women, which is so difficult,

It's you, night, who put to bed the whole of Creation

In a bed of a few hours.

(Awaiting.) In a bed of a few hours

Image, feeble image, and promise and prefiguration of the bed of every hour.

Anticipated realization. Promise kept in advance

Awaiting the bed of every hour.
In which I, the Father, will lay my creation.
O Night, you are night. And all the days together
Will never be day, they will never be anything but several days.
Scattered. The days will never be anything but flashes.
Uncertain flashes, and you, night, you are my great somber light.
I congratulate myself for having made night. The days are isles and
        islands
That pierce and split the sea.
But they have to rest in the deep sea.
They're forced to.
And you too, days, you're forced to as well.
You have to rest in the deep night.
And you, night, you are the deep sea
Upon which St. Paul sailed, not that little lake in Galilee.
All the days are nothing but members
Dismembered members. It's the days that emerge, but even so they
        have to be anchored in the deep water.
In the deep night. Night, my finest invention, it's you who calm, it's
        you who soothe, it's you who bring rest
To aching limbs
All out of joint from the day's work.
It's you who calm, it's you who soothe, it's you who bring rest
To aching hearts
To bruised bodies, to limbs bruised from work, to hearts bruised from
        work
And from daily cares and sorrow.
O Night, o my daughter Night, the most religious of all my daughters
The most reverent.
Of all my daughters, of all my creatures, the most abandoned into my
        hands.
You glorify me in Sleep even more than your Brother, Day, glorifies me
        in Work.
Because in work man only glorifies me by his work.
Whereas in sleep it is I who glorify myself by man's surrender.
And it's more certain, and I know better how to go about it.
Night, you are for man a more nourishing food than bread and wine.

THE PORTAL OF THE MYSTERY OF HOPE

Because the man who eats and drinks, if he doesn't sleep, will not
     profit from his nourishment.
And it will sour and upset his stomach.
But if he sleeps, the bread and wine will become his flesh and blood.
For working. For praying. For sleeping.
Night, you alone dress wounds.
Aching hearts. All out of joint. All torn.
O my dark-eyed daughter, of all my daughters you alone are, and can
     call yourself, my accomplice.
You are in league with me, because you and me, me through you,
Together we cause man to fall into the trap of my arms
And we take him a bit by surprise.
But one takes what one can get. If anyone knows, it's me.
Night, you are the beautiful creation
Of my wisdom.
Night, o my daughter Night, o my silent daughter
At Rebecca's well, at the well of the Samaritan woman[70]
It's you who draw the deepest water
From the deepest well
O night who gently rocks all creatures
Into a restoring sleep.
O night who bathes all wounds
In the only fresh water and in the only deep water
At Rebecca's well, drawn from the deepest well.
Friend of children, friend and sister to the young Hope
O night who dresses all wounds
At the well of the Samaritan woman, you who draw, from the deepest
     well,
The deepest prayer.
O night, o my daughter Night, you who know how to keep silent, o
     my daughter of the beautiful mantle.
You who confer rest and forgetfulness. You who issue a healing balm,
     and silence, and shadow
O my starry night, I created you first.
You who send to sleep, you who already enshroud in an eternal
     Darkness,
All of my most restless creatures,
The fiery steed, the industrious ant,

And man, that monster of unrest.
Night you succeed in quieting man
That well of unrest.
By himself more restless than all of creation put together.
Man, that well of anxiety.
Just as you quiet the water in the well.
O my night with the glorious dress
You gather children and the young Hope
Into the folds of your dress
Though men resist you.
O my beautiful night, I created you first.
And practically before first
O silent one, draped with veils
You who descend on earth as a foretaste
You who scatter by hand, who pour out over the earth
An initial peace
    Forerunner of eternal peace.
An initial rest
    Forerunner of eternal rest.
An initial soothing balm, an initial beatitude
    Forerunner of eternal beatitude.
You who soothe, you who embalm, you who console.
You who bind wounds and injured limbs.
You who silence hearts, you who quiet bodies
Who still aching hearts, aching bodies,
Wrought with pain,
Worn-out limbs, backs broken
With weariness, with care, with (mortal) anxieties,
With sorrow,
You who administer balm to throats torn with bitterness
A cooling balm
O my noble-hearted daughter, I created you first
Practically before first, my great-bosomed daughter
And I knew well what I was doing.
Surely, I knew what I was doing.
You who lay the child in his mother's arms
The child, brightened with a shadow of sleep

Laughing inwardly, laughing secretly because of his confidence in his
     mother.
And in me,
Laughing secretly out of the corner of his serious mouth
You who lay the child, inwardly bursting, overflowing with innocence
And with confidence
In the arms of his mother
You who used to lay the child Jesus every night
In the arms of the Most Holy and Immaculate one.
You who are the turn-sister of hope.[71]
O my daughter, first among all. You who even succeed,
You who occasionally succeed,
You who lay man in the arms of my Providence
My maternal Providence
O my daughter, *glittering and dark,* I salute you
You who restore, you who nourish, you who give rest
O silence of darkness[72]
Such a silence reigned before the creation of anxiety.
Before the beginning of the reign of anxiety
Such a silence will reign, now a silence of light,
When all this anxiety will have been consummated,
When all this anxiety will have been exhausted.
When they will have drawn all the water from the well.
After the consummation, after the exhaustion of all this anxiety
Man's anxiety.
Thus, my daughter, you come early and you come late
For in this reign of anxiety you recall, you commemorate, you
     practically reestablish,
You practically recommence the former Serenity that existed
When my spirit brooded over the waters.
But, my starry daughter, my daughter of the dark mantle, you are also
     very much ahead of your time, you are also precocious.
For you announce, for you represent, for you practically commence in
     advance, every night,
My great Serenity of light
Eternal.
Night, you are holy; Night, you are great; Night, you are beautiful.
Night of the great mantle.

Night, I love you and I salute you and I glorify you and you are my
    great daughter and my creature.
O beautiful night, night of the great mantle, my daughter of the starry
    mantle
You remind me, myself, you remind me of the great silence that existed
Before I had unlocked the firmament of ingratitude.
And you proclaim, even to me, you herald to me the silence that will
    exist
After the end of man's reign, when I will have reclaimed my scepter.
And sometimes I think about it ahead of time, because this man really
    makes a lot of noise.
But above all, Night, you remind me of that night.
And I will remember it eternally.
The ninth hour had sounded. It was in the country of my people of
    Israel.
It was all over. That enormous adventure.
From the sixth hour to the ninth hour there had been a darkness
    covering the entire countryside.
Everything was finished. Let's not talk about it anymore. It hurts me to
    think about it.
My son's incredible descent among men.
Into their midst.
When you think of what they made of him.
Those thirty years that he was a carpenter among men.
Those three years that he was a sort of preacher among men.
A priest.
Those three days when he fell victim to men.
Among men.
Those three nights when he was dead in the midst of men.
Dead among the dead.
Through the centuries of centuries that he's been a host among men.
This incredible adventure was finished.
The adventure that has tied my hands, God, for all eternity.
The adventure by which my Son has tied my hands.
Tying the hands of my justice for eternally, untying the hands of my
    mercy for eternally.[73]
And against my justice, inventing a new justice.
A justice of love. A justice of Hope. Everything was finished.

THE PORTAL OF THE MYSTERY OF HOPE

Everything that was necessary. As it had to be. As my prophets had
    foretold it. The veil of the sanctuary had been torn in two,
    from top to bottom.
The earth had shook; rocks had been split.
Tombs had been opened, and many of the bodies of saints that had
    died rose again.
And around the ninth hour my Son had uttered
The cry that will never fade. Everything was finished. The soldiers had
    returned to their barracks.
Laughing and joking because another task was finished.
One more guard duty that they'd no longer have to make.
One centurion alone remained, and a few men.
Just a simple little post to guard the insignificant tree.
The gallows where my Son was hanging.
Only a few women had remained.
His Mother was there.
And perhaps a few disciples as well, beyond that we can't be sure.
Now every man has the right to bury his own son.
Every man on earth, if the great misfortune befalls him
Not to have died before his son. And I alone, God,
My hands tied by this adventure,
I alone, father at that moment like so many fathers,
I alone was unable to bury my son.
It was then, o night, that you arrived.
O my daughter, my most precious among them all, and it is still before
    my eyes and it will remain before my eyes for all eternity
It was then, o Night, that you came and, in a great shroud, you buried
The Centurion and his Romans,
The Virgin and the holy women,
And that mountain, and that valley, upon which the evening was
    descending,
And my people of Israel and sinners and, with them, he who was
    dying, he who had died for them

And the men sent by Joseph of Arimathea who were already
    approaching
Bearing the white shroud.[74]

NOTES AND VARIATIONS

1. This dedication is similar to that which opens *The Mystery of the Charity of Joan of Arc* and which is addressed to Péguy's friend Marcel Baudouin, who died July 25, 1896. This time, *The Portal* is dedicated to another friend, Eddy Marix, who died August 3, 1908, after having written a play in five acts and in verse, *La Tragédie de Tristan et Yseut*, published April 20, 1905, in the *Cahiers de la Quinzaine* (fifteenth cahier from the sixth series).

   The similarity between the two dedications lies in the formula of the opening: "Not only in memory of, but dedicated to," which implies that Péguy is dedicating his work to someone who is alive even though he may no longer belong to this earth. The relationship between friends continues after death and, just as at Mass, the one who remains makes an offering to the one who has entered into eternity.

   Following the same liturgical spirit, the two dedications then place themselves within the calendar of the feasts of Christ and of the Church by recalling Christmas and the Epiphany in the first case, and Palm Sunday, Easter, All Saints' Day, and All Souls' Day in the second.

   Both close finally with the preparation for a special commemoration: the "five-hundredth anniversary of the birth of Joan of Arc, which will come on the Feast of the Epiphany of the year 1912." Joan of Arc is believed to have been born January 6, 1412. By relating her birth to the Feast of the Kings, that is, the Feast of the Epiphany, Péguy joins the temporal with the eternal, secular history with sacred history.

2. Madame Gervaise, the only protagonist in *The Portal*, is a twenty-five-year-old Franciscan nun. Péguy created this character with his initial version of *Joan of Arc* in 1897. In *The Mystery of the Charity of Joan of Arc*, he greatly increased her role by granting her the enormous speech that includes the recitation of the Passion. With *The Portal*, Madame Gervaise monopolizes the entire text, and, more or less, continues to do so in *The Mystery of the Holy Innocents*.

   We have scarcely begun to examine the reasons for such a startling promotion. Renée Balibar's meticulous study ("Sur le personnage de Madame Gervaise dans Péguy") permits us to establish that the name most likely comes from Péguy's readings at school as a child (the books of G. Bruno) and that Madame Gervaise was, in some capacity, a young teacher responsible for instructing Joan in the Christian mysteries.

But we may still wonder why Péguy made her a Franciscan nun, belonging to the reform introduced by Colette de Corbie. And yet the first pages of *The Portal* emphasize this aspect with force, because they are a reprise of the Canticle of Creatures, which itself takes up the biblical theme of God revealing himself through his Creation.

3. In her memoirs concerning her brother Pierre, Germaine Péguy recounts that the evocation of the "kingly eagle who has a wingspan of at least two meters" comes no doubt from the reading of the author's young son, who had a passionate interest in ornithology (*L'Amitié Charles Péguy,* no. 16 (October–December 1981): 230).

4. One cannot help but think that the "little girl hope," the image governing the whole poem, was inspired by a real-life little girl: Germaine, Péguy's second child. She was then nine years old.

5. An excerpt from the *Catéchisme d'Orléans,* by Fr. J. Martineau. Péguy used this book when he took his catechism course at Saint-Aignan, given by Fr. Bardet, the parish priest.

6. In saying "my child," Madame Gervaise addresses herself to Joan of Arc, who will be her silent and attentive listener from the beginning to the end of *The Portal.* This expression issues often from the mouth of the Franciscan nun, reminding us that this vast monologue is situated within an even larger dramatic whole (cf., e.g., pp. 7, 41, 45, 52, 57, 62, 67, 68, 71, 75, 77, 78, 86, 89, 90).

7. The *"uphill path, sandy and troublesome":* a quotation from *Le Coche et la mouche,* a fable by Jean de la Fontaine (VII-8).

8. With this image of the woodcutter who works in the forest during the winter, Péguy is certainly recalling one of his great-great-grandparents, the grandfather of his maternal grandmother Etiennette Quéré. In *Pierre, commencement d'une vie bourgeoise,* the author recounts that this ancestor "was a woodcutter and chopped down beautiful trees" in the forests of Gennetines, in Bourbonnais (*Oeuvres en prose 1898–1908* [Pléiade, 1959], 1219).

   The woodcutter's three children are Péguy's three children: Marcel, who was born September 10, 1898; Germaine, who was born September 7, 1901; and Pierre, who was born June 25, 1903.

9. Pierre Péguy turned seven in 1910. This tells us that *The Portal* was written between June 1910 and June 1911, confirming our supposition that this *Mystery* was finished several months before its publication, most likely during the winter of 1910–1911 (*Oeuvres poétiques complètes,* [Pléiade, 1975]).

10. "They are sons of France and of Lorraine": The poem requires that the woodcutter and his children be contemporaries of Joan of Arc, from the fifteenth century, and thus they are from Lorraine just as she is.

11. *"Dans les siècles des siècles,"* translated here, and elsewhere throughout the text, as "through centuries of centuries," is usually rendered in the English versions of prayers as "world without end," or simply "forever." The more literal translation has been kept as being faithful to Péguy's imagery. [Translator's note]

12. One among these names from Lorraine — Sévin, Chénin, Jouffin, Damrémont —

is the name of one of Péguy's friends, an author that was born in Lorraine. Emile Chénin (1870–1918) published several works in the *Cahiers* under the pseudonym Emile Moselly: *L'Aube fraternelle* (IV-2, October 23, 1902), *Jean des brebis ou le livre de la misère* (V-15, May 1, 1904), *Les Retours* (VII-19, July 24, 1906), *Le Rouet d'ivoire* (IX-4, November 12, 1907). *Jean des brebis* was awarded the Goncourt prize in 1907.

Later, with Ollendorff Press, Moselly published several other novels that Péguy loved: *Joson Meunier* (1910), *Fils de gueux* (1912), and *Les Etudiants* (1914). From 1899 to 1910, he was a literature professor at the lycée d'Orléans, where he had Maurice Genevoix as a student (cf. Alfred Saffrey, *Correspondance Péguy-Moselly*, Cahiers de l'Amitié Charles Péguy no. XVIII [1966], and Jean Bastaire, "L'école réaliste des Cahiers: Lavergne, Moselly, Hamp, Thierry," in the *Courrier d'Orléans*, no. 35 [August 1971]: 3-21).

13. The French have two different words to distinguish due pride *(fierté)* from the sin of pride *(orgueil)*. Here, the sin of pride is distinguished by the capital letter. [Tr. note]

14. "He'll have lost the taste for bread": an idiomatic expression for having died. [Tr. note]

15. A French proverb. [Tr. note]

16. "Their domed brow, all freshly washed and clean from baptism": Péguy's own children were not baptized. Here we can sense the regret of their father, who had a civil marriage with a non-Catholic spouse. She would not accept the Christian sacraments because of the religious obligations they implied.

17. *"On the imitation of Jesus"*: the title of a famous work by Thomas A. Kempis, *De imitatione Jesu Christi*, contemporary with Joan of Arc and a boundless source of piété, as much in the seventeenth century (Corneille's translation) as in the nineteenth century (Lamennais's translation).

18. During the time that he was writing this page, Péguy had, not three sick children, but one sick child: his youngest son Pierre had an infectious flu, which confined him to bed for three months during the spring of 1911, and which threatened to leave him paralyzed (*Lettres et entretiens*, collected by Marcel Péguy [Ed. de Paris, 1954], 78). The following year the same child came down with two other serious conditions: typhoid fever in February and diptheria in August (*Lettres*, 117, 133).

19. "He hadn't told his wife about it. . . . It's much better not to make such a fuss over it./And to have peace in the home": with Péguy's wife being an unbeliever, and with the problem of the children's baptism already having caused tensions in the family, we can understand that the poet would have preferred to keep silent about his recourse to the Blessed Virgin.

20. "Giving them a kiss . . . right on the crown of their heads": in her memoirs concerning her brother Pierre, Germaine Péguy notes that he was the one who would thus present himself to his father for a kiss (*L'Amitié Charles Péguy*, no. 16 [October–December 1981]: 231-32).

21. "It's infinitely ever-better": this could have been translated, following Péguy's

French, as "infinitely more better." As it stands, it is perhaps a little less shocking to the ear. [Tr. note]

22. "Admire the wisdom of this man": Madame Gervaise seems here to appeal more directly to Joan, her silent listener, and also when she says "I swear to you" (p. 38) or "I'm going to explain to you" (p. 45).

23. A French proverb. [Tr. note]

24. Péguy seems not to know St. Marcel, a relatively well-known pope and martyr, who died in 309 and whose feast falls on January 16. In the breviary that the poet owned and read, he would have been able to find details about St. Marcel's brief pontificate (308–309). There was also another St. Marcel, a bishop of Paris, who died in 430 and is buried in the suburb that bears his name.

   Marcel, Péguy's oldest son, received his name from his deceased maternal uncle, Marcel Baudouin.

   St. Germaine (1579–1601), the namesake of Péguy's only daughter, lived in the southwest of France during the religious wars. She was canonized in 1867; her feast is celebrated on June 15. Her history would have held some interest for Péguy if he had wished to study it, since she was a shepherdess like Joan of Arc and died scarcely older than the young saint.

   These two would have formed a nice trio with St. Geneviève (422–502), who was also a shepherdess. She is the patronness of Paris, and her feast is celebrated on January 3. Péguy had a special reason for calling Geneviève *"our great friend"*: she represents a very dear friend of his, Geneviève Favre, the mother of Jacques Maritain.

   As for St. Germain, the poet chose the bishop of Auxerre (378–448) because of his ties with St. Geneviève. He could just as well have recalled a bishop of Paris, who lived in the sixth century and is buried in the church of Saint-Germain-des-Prés, which is dedicated to him.

25. St. Peter, the first head of the apostolic community and the first pope, tortured to death in Rome in 64, had earlier denied Christ during the night of his Passion. By saying that "it's probably better not to talk too much about it," Madame Gervaise is not seeking to hide this betrayal, atoned for by blood, but rather, she incites all the Christians who have lost their fidelity to Christ to a personal humility, just as she did when she recalled the scene to Joan in *The Mystery of the Charity* ("how many cocks crow for us; the race has not thereby perished").

   Pierre, Péguy's youngest son, no doubt received his name in reference to Pierre Baudouin, the pseudonym Péguy himself adopted for his first *Joan of Arc*, in union with his brother-in-law Marcel, who had recently died. Here, Péguy found a new way to commemorate the deceased.

   "And the Gates of Hell shall not prevail against it. Tu es Petrus, et super hanc petram": a quotation from the Gospel according to St. Matthew (14:18), the Latin part coming before the French part in the text of the Vulgate.

26. The Parable of the Lost Sheep, following the Gospel according to St. Luke (15:1-7).

27. *"Queen of the heavens, earthly ruler/Empress of the infernal swamplands"*: the beginning

of the *Ballade à Notre Dame* by François Villon (the first verse is cited again on p. 51).

28. "To she who is Mary/Because she is full of grace": a paraphrase of the first four lines of the "Hail Mary," borrowed from the Gospel according to St. Luke (1:28, 42).

29. "As pure as Eve before the first sin": here Péguy confesses his belief in the Immaculate Conception of Mary. He expressed the same belief to Stanislas Fumet in these terms: "Every question concerning the spiritual and the temporal, the eternal and the carnal, gravitates around a central point which continually occupies my thoughts and is the cornerstone of my religion. That point is the Immaculate Conception" (*Hommage à Charles Péguy,* collected works [Gallimard, 1929], 37).

   "See that you do not harm one of these little ones . . . etc.": a quotation from the Gospel according to St. Matthew (18:10-14).

30. "The will before your Father": Péguy translates the Vulgate ("Voluntas ante Patrem vestrum") literally. [Tr. note]

31. *"Et erraverit una ex eis":* and if one of them lost its way (Matt. 18:12). The complete text reads: "If someone had a hundred sheep, and if one of them lost its way, wouldn't he leave the ninety-nine in the mountains and go look for the one that was lost."

32. *"Blessed among women":* the third line from the "Hail Mary" (Luke 1:42).

33. The extensive use here of the masculine and feminine pronouns to distinguish between the body and the soul, plus the use of certain expressions normally attributed to people *(elle pour soi),* seems to justify a shift to personification in the English. [Tr. note]

34. *"The very body of Jesus":* Péguy underscores the radical character of the incarnation of the Son of God, who has truly assumed a body similar to that of all humans. Thus, by the body of Jesus, all humans are united with God.

35. "Atoned for by the flesh and by the Blood": the Blood of the Eucharistic chalice.

36. *"See that you do not harm a single one of these little ones . . .":* a quotation from the Gospel according to St. Matthew (18:10). The same line is repeated at p. 57.

37. "In-carnal-ation": *encharnellement* in the French. [Tr. note]

38. *"Ego sum via, veritas et vita":* a quotation from the Gospel according to St. John (14:6).

39. *"In monte":* an allusion to the Sermon on the Mount (Matt. 5-7 and Luke 7:12-49).

40. "O misery, o misfortune": this is reminiscent of the *Sacré,* a poem by Victor Hugo (*Les Châtiments,* V, 1). In this poem, we find the expression "O sorrow, o misery" repeated seventeen times, and an eighteenth and final time, we find it reversed, "O misery, o sorrow." Péguy comments on this passage at length in *Clio* (*Oeuvres en prose 1909–1914* [Pléiade, 1961], 182-200).

41. "The vase breaks . . . and it doesn't lose a single drop of its liqueur": this is reminiscent of the *Vase brisé* by Sully-Prudhomme (*Stances et poèmes*). In his youth, Péguy loved this poet, who possessed a profound sense of justice and human suffering.

42. "He didn't waste his time and he didn't take pains": *la peine,* in French, can mean

either sadness\sorrow or effort\trouble. Though this phrase would be more accurately translated as "he didn't waste his time and effort," "he didn't take pains" seems to lend itself better to Péguy's play on words two lines later. [Tr. note]

43. "Who try to see something where it's not": The French expression reads literally, "Who always look for noon at two o'clock." [Tr. note]

44. "Now, when your mother sends you to run an errand at the bakery": Madame Gervaise once again addresses Joan, whom she compares to a young girl in Péguy's time. It is unlikely, however, that there would have been a bakery in Domrémy at the beginning of the fifteenth century.

45. "For eternally": Péguy bends the usual rules of grammar here in order to achieve his desired effect. [Tr. note]

46. The order of the Latin has been rearranged for the sake of juxtaposition. Normally, *pereat* would fall between *ut* and *unus*. [Tr. note]

47. The Parable of the Lost Sheep, as it is recounted in the Gospel according to St. Luke (15:1-7).

48. *"Christ is risen":* a formula from the Easter liturgy.

49. "The body of Jesus, in every church, isn't it . . . at the mercy of the least of the soldiers": an allusion to the scandals of the Hundred Year War (the pillaging of churches, the desecration of the hosts). In *The Mystery of the Charity,* Joan had already said to Madame Gervaise: "Don't you realize that the soldiers are carousing around with the most holy consecrated hosts?"

50. St. Loup (or Leu) is a popular saint in the region of Orléans, Péguy's homeland. We also find a cult of this saint in Normandy and in the Paris Basin. Could he have been the bishop of Troyes, from the fifth century, who defended his village against Attila, or even the bishop of Lyon, from the sixth century, who presided at the regional council at Orléans? It is more likely that he was the archbishop of Sens, from the seventh century, who was exiled by Clotaire II and to whom a great number of sanctuaries have been dedicated.

"The ten silver coins which is like saying ten Parisian pounds": an allusion to the Parable of the Ten Silver Coins, as it is told in the Gospel according to St. Luke (15:8-10). The Parisian pound (= a pound from Paris) was a coin used during the Ancien Régime that was worth twenty sous and was eventually abolished under Louis XIV.

51. *"Advocata nostra":* our advocate. A quotation from the liturgical hymn *Salve regina,* which seems to date back to the sixth century.

52. The Parable of the Ten Silver Coins, taken from the Gospel according to St. Luke (15:8-10).

53. "The parable of the lost child": an allusion to the Parable of the Prodigal Son, as found in the Gospel according to St. Luke (15:11-32). Of all the parables, this one was most dear to Péguy. Not only does he meditate on it in *The Portal* and in *The Holy Innocents,* but it also holds a central place in *La Ballade du coeur,* as it has been reconstructed by Julie Sabiani. Moreover, at one point Péguy had proposed, and even

NOTES AND VARIATIONS

begun, to write *The Mystery of the Prodigal Son,* which he abandoned after only a few hours of work (*Oeuvres poétiques complètes* [Pléiade, 1975]).

54. "Throughout the thirteen and fourteen centuries that they've served, and throughout two thousand years": Madame Gervaise counts the years in relation to the fifteenth century, in which she herself lived, but also in relation to the twentieth century, in which Péguy lived.

55. *"Then he said: A man had two sons"*: the first line of the Parable of the Prodigal Son (Luke 15:11). This line is then taken up as a refrain (cf. pp. 94, 96, 97, 98, 113, 121).

56. "Once this word of hope has bitten into his heart/Into his believing or unbelieving heart,/No pleasure will ever more be able to erase/Its teeth-marks./ . . . She thus accompanies man into his greatest follies": an allusion to the crisis that was eating away at Péguy during these years. In spite of his love for a young woman, Blanche Raphaël, Péguy denied his passion and, like Pauline in Corneille's *Polyeucte,* whom he greatly admired, he preferred "honor" to "happiness."

"It is not God's will/That a single one of these little ones should perish": once again, a quotation from the Gospel according to St. Matthew (18:14).

57. The personification of the word of hope in this image is less dramatic in the French because there all nouns take masculine or feminine pronouns as a rule. [Tr. note]

58. "As far as man might stray, far from the hearth, far from the heart . . . into the shamefulness of his heart": another allusion to Péguy's passion for Blanche Raphaël.

59. "And I myself can't get over it/My grace must, indeed, be great": Marcel Péguy suggests interposing here a variation that resumes and develops the affirmation "I myself can't get over it" (*Oeuvres poétiques complètes* [Pléiade, 1957], 1512-14):

> I myself can't get over it, says God. I never would've guessed
> that I'd have been so successful:
> I know why it is. I know my catechism very well, thank you.
> It's all because of this little hope. She's a virtue that relates immediately
> to me (*There was a great procession. At the head of the procession marched*
> the three Theological Virtues).
> It's all because of this child. I know her well.
> She's insatiable. *I will give them my grace in this world and my glory*
> *in the next.*
> *Because I promised it to them and because I am supremely faithful*
> *in my promises.*
> This is how I am committed to them.
> And it's not my will,
> *Non est posita ante me voluntas,*
> *It is not my will*
> *That a single one of these little ones should perish.*
> All of it is this child's fault. She went and told it to everyone.
> You can never say anything in front of children.
>
> She went and told the whole of creation the greatest of my secrets.

Children play with secrets like they play catch with a ball.
What carelessness. But she had the right. She's a child.
I was the one who was careless. I shouldn't have let go in front of a child
My greatest secret. *A man had two sons.* She went, like a child,
    she went and told all the other children.
A secret for grown-ups.
And now these poor children have hope buried so deeply in their hearts
That nothing will ever more be able to pull it out.

There must be a secret in this child,
Says God,
Some secret of her strength. She can get where none of the others can reach.
She can do what none of the others can.
There must be a secret in this child.
A special strength.
Among all my daughters, the virtues.
She is one of my greatest daughters,
(Out of all of them, I have three great ones).
She succeeds where the others fail.
But her secret, says God, heavens it's not tricky, I too know
    all of the world's secrets.
I am within all the secrets of creation.
My gaze rests within.
My gaze is the light itself.
That enlightens.
Her great secret, why yes, it's precisely that she is a child.

60. "On the banks of the Meuse/Beautiful water from Lorraine": the scene is situated in the countryside, not far from Domrémy, where Joan is taking her sheep out to pasture.

61. "Sorrowful gardens of souls have grown there/Which have suffered without disrupting the arrangement/The most difficult martyrdom/Without destroying the order": once again, an allusion to Péguy's love for Blanche Raphaël and his resistance to this passion.

62. The uncle he speaks of here is Albert Badouin, the brother of Charlotte, Péguy's wife, and of Marcel, his deceased friend. While Péguy wrote *The Portal*, Albert Badouin was living in his household.

63. *"Woe to he who is lukewarm"*: an allusion to the verse from Revelation: "So, because you are lukewarm, neither hot nor cold, I will spit you out of my mouth" (3:16).

64. Playing on the French word for weed, *la mauvaise herbe,* Péguy suggests that *la mauvaise nature* grows *la mauvaise herbe.* The pun is lost in English. [Tr. note]

65. *"A man had two sons"*: Péguy recalls the Parable of the Prodigal Son (Luke 15:11), to which he includes an allusion to the Parable of the Weeds and the Wheat (Matt. 13:24-30).

NOTES AND VARIATIONS

66. "To take the grown-ups for a ride": literally, "to make the grown-ups walk." In French, the expression would mean idiomatically, "to fool the grown-ups," playing on the sense of deception implicit in disappointment. The English expression is an attempt to capture both meanings. [Tr. note]

67. "When Jesus worked at his father's shop": Péguy here sketches the celebration of the private life of Jesus, the universal source of sanctity, which he will develop further in *Un nouveau théologien M. Laudet,* written at the same time as the end of *The Portal.*

68. *"A man had two sons":* another reminder of the Parable of the Prodigal Son (Luke 15:11), to which Péguy includes, this time, an allusion to the Parable of the Workers in the Vineyard (Matt. 20:1-16).

69. "He who sleeps, prays": a variation of the French proverb, *Qui dort, dine* (He who sleeps, eats). [Tr. note]

70. "At Rebecca's well, at the well of the Samaritan woman": allusions to an episode in the Old Testament, the marriage of Isaac and Rebecca (Gen. 24), and to an episode in the New Testament, the conversation between Jesus and the Samaritan woman (John 4:1-42).

71. "The turn-sister of hope": the expression "turn-sister" (soeur-tourière) apparently refers to the gadget in the wall of cloistered convents through which objects are passed by *turning* a cylinder which is half cut away. The sister who attends it, whether on the outside or the inside, is the turn-sister.

72. *"Glittering and dark . . ./O silence of darkness":* this is undoubtedly a reference to Victor Hugo. In *Victor-Marie, comte Hugo,* Péguy remarks on "this seemingly eternal lease by which Victor Hugo has secured himself the exclusive property, use, and enjoyment of the word *ombre* [darkness\shadow] in the singular and plural, especially as a rhyme. His rhyming with *ombre(s)* has often acheived beautifull effects" (*Oeuvres en prose 1909–1914* [Pléiade, 1961], 713).

73. "For eternally": Péguy stretched the rules of grammar here, presumably, to give the act of tying God's hands a sense of being continuous, rather than once and for all. [Tr. note]

74. Joseph of Arimathea was a respected Jew and disciple of Jesus who came to ask Pilate for the body of the crucified so that he could bury it in his own tomb. This generosity inspires Madame Gervaise, in *The Mystery of the Charity,* to make the following remark:

> You could lend out your donkey to someone to go to the market.
> You could lend out your tub to someone to do the laundry.
> . . . .
> But to lend out your sepulchre
> That's out of the ordinary.

"Bearing the white shroud": Marcel Péguy gives the following as a variation of the ending that Péguy himself, with a pair of scissors, had cut from his manuscript in order to have a more dramatic finish (*Oeuvres poétiques complètes* [Pléiade, 1957], 1514-15):

> O night, you had no need to go ask Pilate his permission.
>> That's why I love you and I salute you.
> And among all creatures I glorify you and among all creatures you glorify me
> And you give me honor and glory
> Because you sometimes obtain that which is most difficult in all the world,
> Man's surrender,
> Man's abandonment into my hands.
> I know man well. Indeed, I made him.
> You can still ask a lot from him. He's not too bad.
> When you know how to handle him, you can still ask a lot from him.
> You can still get a lot from him. And God knows whether my grace
> Knows how to handle him, whether with my grace
> I know how to handle him. You can still ask a lot of kindness from him,
>> a lot of charity, a lot of sacrifice.
> But what you can't ask from him, by God, is a little hope.
> A little confidence, just a little relaxation,
> A little postponing, a little abandonment into my hands.
> A little surrender. He's so uptight all the time.
> Now you, my daughter night, you occasionally succeed,
>> you sometimes obtain this.
> From rebellious man.
> So that he consents, this man, so that he yields a little to me.
> So that he stretches his poor limbs out a bit on a bed of rest.
> So that he eases his aching heart a bit on a bed of rest.
> So that his head, above all, stops working. His head works only too much.
>> And he believes that's work, when his head churns like that.
> So that his ideas quit marching around, and quit bouncing around
>> in his head, and quit rattling.
> Like seeds in an empty gourd. His ideas, for what they're worth.
> Now you, daughter night, you alone in this
> You are the only one who can accomplish this, I know, you alone can obtain
> What all the others cannot obtain: a little relief, a little alleviation
> A little renunciation.
> This most difficult renunciation of all renunciations
> A little of this surrender.
> At this, my daughter, you are the most accomplished
> The only one who can accomplish that which is most difficult.
> The only thing that's difficult. They say that man is greedy.
> They don't know him well. Yes, man is greedy.

CHRONOLOGY

1873   *January 7:* Charles Pierre Péguy is born in Orléans, 50, rue du faubourg Bourgogne, as the only son of Désiré Péguy, a carpenter. Désiré Péguy was born in Saint-Jean-de-Braye, February 21, 1846, from a family of winegrowers. On January 8, 1872, in Orléans, Désiré Péguy married Cécile Quéré, born in Moulins, November 22, 1846, the illegitimate daughter of Etiennette Quéré, of Gennetines origin, in Allier. Péguy is ten months old when his father dies, November 18, 1873. His mother learns the trade of mending chairs.

1879   *October:* Enters elementary school, which is annexed to the Ecole Normale for teachers, in Loiret, 72, rue du faubourg Bourgogne. His performance at school is remarkable.

1884   *July:* Graduates from elementary school.
        October: Enters secondary school, a professional school at the time, in the cloister of Sainte-Croix.

1885   *Easter:* Enters for his sixth year [French schools count the years in reverse — Tr.] at the lycée in Orléans, thanks to a municipal grant for half-boarders, which he receives from M. Naudy, the director of the Ecole Normale in Loiret.

1885–   From his sixth year to his year in philosophy, Péguy exhibits
1891   brilliant and rigorous studies. He follows a course in religious instruction until his second year.

1891   *July 21:* Obtains a baccalaureate in letters.
        October: Enters the lycée of Lakanal, in Sceaux, with a grant from the State.

1892   *July:* Fails his entrance exams for the Ecole Normale.
        September: Enlists before his time in the 131st regiment of the infantry in Orléans, taking advantage of the law that makes him a "one-year volunteer."

1893   *July:* Fails his entrance exams for the Ecole Normale a second time.

October: With a grant from the administration committee, Péguy enters the college of Sainte-Barbe in Paris as an intern, where he is able to take courses in advanced rhetoric at the Lycée Louis-le-Grand. He strikes up a deep friendship with Marcel Baudouin.

1894   *August:* Passes his entrance exams for the Ecole Normale, ranked sixth. Travels to Orange to attend a performance of Sophocles' *Antigone* and *Oedipus Rex.*
November: Obtains a licentiate in letters, with a mention in philosophy.
His first year at the Ecole Normale.

1895   *May:* Becomes a socialist.
End of October: Travels to Domrémy and Vaucouleurs.
November: Takes a leave of absence from school for the year. Returns to Orléans, where he learns printing, founds a socialist center — the "Groupe d'études sociales d'Orléans," and begins to write his first *Joan of Arc.*

1896   *June:* Marcel Baudouin visits Péguy at Orléans; the conception of *Marcel, premier dialogue de la cité harmonieuse.*
July 25: Marcel Baudouin dies.
November: Péguy returns to the Ecole Normale for his second year of studies.

1897   *February: Revue socialiste* publishes the first article signed C.P.: "Un économiste socialiste, M. Léon Walras." Six other articles will appear in the same review under the pseudonyms Pierre Deloire and Jacques Deloire; one of these is the manifesto "De la cité socialiste," which appears in August.
October 28: Marries Charlotte François Baudouin, born in 1879, the sister of his deceased friend. They move to a house at 7, rue de l'Estrapade.
November: Having withdrawn from the Ecole Normale, Péguy is given a teaching grant along with permission to audit courses from Georges Lyon and, beginning February 1898, from Henri Bergson.
December: Publication of *Joan of Arc,* a drama comprising three plays in twenty-four acts, under the signature of Marcel and Pierre Baudouin. This trilogy traces the entire life of Joan of Arc: her childhood, the battles, and the trial.

1898   *February:* Participates in the campaign for Dreyfus by paying a visit to Zola and Jaurès, and by signing petitions for a revision in the journals *L'Aurore* and *La Petite République.*

May: Founds a socialist bookstore, called the "Librairie Georges Bellais," located at 17 rue Cujas, in the Latin Quarter. To do so, he spends his wife's dowry of 40,000 francs.

June: At the Librairie Georges Bellais, he publishes *Marcel, premier dialogue de la cité harmonieuse,* under the pseudonym Pierre Baudouin. Here, Péguy expounds his ideas about the utopian cité for which he is preparing.

August: Fails his exam for teaching in philosophy.

September 10: Marcel Péguy, the writer's first child, is born.

November: Péguy undertakes the writing of *Pierre, commencement d'une vie bourgeoise,* an autobiography, which he signs as Pierre Baudouin, but which he leaves unfinished. It is eventually published in 1931 by his son Marcel Péguy.

November 15, 1889–January 15, 1899: La Revue blanche publishes a series of five articles in which, under the pseudonym Jacques Laubier, he fights for Dreyfus. In one of them, he opposes the patriotism of an International Socialist to the League of French Nationalists.

1899   *February 1–November 15:* In *La Revue blanche,* Péguy publishes under his own name eleven articles in which he denounces the socialists' slowness in taking part in the defense of Dreyfus and, in this battle, supports Jaurès against Guesde.

July: Moves to Saint-Clair, near Orsay.

August: Following financial difficulties, the Librairie Georges Bellais is converted into a bookselling and publishing society. Lucien Herr and Léon Blum have a place on the administrative board. Péguy is henceforward assigned to publishing.

December: Because a congress of socialist organizations had voted for the institution of a central control of the socialist press, Péguy decides to leave and publish his *cahiers* of documentation and reflection in full liberty. He breaks with Lucien Herr, who treats him as an anarchist.

1900   *January 5:* The first number of the *Cahiers de la Quinzaine* [Fortnightly Journals — Tr.]. Its office gives its provisional address as 19, rue des Fossés-Saint-Jacques, at the home of

Tharaud. In the form of a manifesto, the *Lettre du provincial* gives a single order: "tell the truth."

February–April: In *De la grippe, Encore de la grippe,* and *Toujours de la grippe,* Péguy ridicules the socialist demogogy and rejects the Catholic teaching on hell (*Cahier* I-4, I-6, I-7).

November: The office is moved to 16, rue de la Sorbonne, in the Ecole's building for social studies. Péguy takes André Bourgeois on as an administrator.

November 29: The first *cahier* of the second series; each series covers one school year rather than a calendar year.

1902   *March 2:* In *Casse-cou,* Péguy warns Jaurès about binding socialism to a particular system of philosophy (*Cahier* II-7).

July 15: Péguy's family moves to Orsay, rue des Sablons.

September 7: Germaine Péguy, the writer's second child, is born.

October: The office of the *Cahiers* moves definitively to 8, rue de la Sorbonne.

December 5: In *De la raison,* Péguy takes a stand against any state-established metaphysics and formulates the right use of reason (*Cahier* III-4).

1902   *April 5:* His article *Personnalités* pleads for the necessity of incarnating ideas in people (*Cahier* III-12).

November 4: In connection with a novel by A. Lavergne about teachers, *De Jean Coste* protests suffering and poverty (*Cahier* IV-3).

December 4: In *Les Récentes Oeuvres de Zola,* Péguy expresses regret that, in his latest novels, the author of *J'accuse* celebrates the conquests of the bourgeoisie more so than the socialist gospel (*Cahier* IV-5).

1903   *May 12:* Péguy offers a critique of the system of parliament in *Débats parlementaires* (*Cahier* IV-18).

June 16: Reprise politique parlementaire carries on an analysis of the deterioration of the Dreyfus Affair (*Cahier* IV-20).

June 25: Pierre Péguy, the writer's third child, is born.

1904   *January–February:* In three conferences on *Political Anarchy,* Péguy distinguishes between "the authority of command" and "the authority of competence" (these texts are published in 1969 in the *Oeuvres posthumes,* edited by Jacques Viard).

March 1: L'Avertissement au cahier Mangasarian establishes that a revolution is a deepening of tradition (*Cahier* V-11).

October 30: Zangwill opens a long critique of positivistic historical methods (*Cahier* VI-3).

November 8: Un essai de monople describes what could turn into a totalitarianism from the left (*Cahier* VI-4).

1905   *January 29: La Délation aux Droits de l'homme* condemns combism [the ensemble of the political ideas of the minister Combes (1835–1921) and his partisans, largely concerned with ridding the State of any Catholic influence — Tr.] (*Cahier* VI-9).

July–September: The threat of the Germans inspires Péguy to write *Notre patrie* (*Cahier* VII-3) and *Par ce demi-clair matin* (published in 1952). He also writes *L'Esprit de système,* in which he attacks ideological terrorism (published in 1953).

December 12: Les Suppliantes parallèles shows the present significance of the Greek tragedy and suggests that one should not confuse revolt with revolution (*Cahier* VII-7).

December 26: Louis de Gonzagne is an exhortation to a calm vigilance in the face of the eventuality of a war (*Cahier* VII-8).

1906   *July–September:* Continuing the analyses begun in 1904 with *Zangwill,* Péguy writes *De la situation faite à l'histoire et à la sociologie dans les temps modernes* (*Cahier* VIII-13), *De la situation faite au parti intellectuel dans le monde moderne* (VIII-5), *Cahiers de la Quinzaine* (VIII-11), and *Brunetière* (published in 1953), in which he deepens his critique of the heirs of Taine and of Renan.

1907   *March:* Péguy confides to Jacques Maritain his new progression toward the Christian faith.

July–September: Carrying on his investigations of 1904 and 1906, *De la situation faite au parti intellectuel devant les accidents de la gloire temporelle* ends with a prose poem about the glory of Paris, of the Beauce, and of the Loire Valley (*Cahier* IX-1).

December: Un poète l'a dit adds new arguments to his critique of modern metaphysics (published in 1953).

1908   *January:* Péguy's family moves into the Maison des Pins, in Lozère, part of the Chevreuse valley.

Spring–summer: Deuxième élégie XXX contrasts the sage with the philosopher, the classicist with the romantic, and celebrates the Ile-de-France (published in 1953).

September 10: Suffering from a serious illness and in the midst of profound distress, Péguy confides his newfound Catholic faith to Joseph Lotte.

October–December: The beginning of his *Thèse*, a reflection on the philosophy of science, in which the author contrasts Auguste Comte's three stages with his own theory of the age of empiricism, the age of science, and the age of competence (published in 1953).

December: Jacques Maritain tries in vain to persuade Péguy to find a spiritual director.

1909   *June 16:* He submits the exact title of his thesis to the Sorbonne, *De la situation faite à l'histoire dans la philosophie générale du monde moderne.* This work will never be completed.

June 20: A tragic ten-year assessment of the management of the *Cahiers, A nos amis, à nos abonnés (Cahier* X-13) continues with *Nous sommes des vaincus* (published in 1953).

July: A tense intervention by Maritain, who tries to persuade Mme. Péguy to have the children baptized.

July–August: Péguy begins his dialogues on history, a project that will continue until 1913, and will not be published until after his death. *Le Dialogue de l'histoire et de l'âme charnelle* is a pamphlet arguing against the "mistake of mysticism" made by Christians who have forgotten the temporal (published in 1955 with the title *Véronique*). *Le Dialogue de l'histoire et de l'âme païen* combines a new critique of historical methods with a meditation on aging and death (published in 1917 with the title *Clio*).

1910   *January 16: The Mystery of the Charity of Joan of Arc* takes up and amplifies the first *Joan of Arc's* questioning about hell, and suggests a response in its contemplation of the Passion of Christ, a passage written in free verse (*Cahier* XI-6).

July 12: Notre jeunesse gives a review of the Dreyfus Affair and, by means of Bernard-Lazare's image, shows the degeneration of *la mystique* into *la politique* [For Péguy, *la mystique* signifies a whole ensemble of spiritual values, including those of the ancient world as much as of the Christian world. — Tr.] (*Cahier* XI-12). "Every party lives by its *mystique* and dies by its *politique*."

July 30: The marriage of Blanche Raphaël, a frequenter of the circles of the *Cahiers,* for whom Péguy experiences a love that is painfully overcome.

October 23: Victor-Marie, comte Hugo recalls Péguy's vine-growing ancestors, reiterates the parallel between Corneille and Racine, and sees in Hugo a pagan prophet of Jesus (*Cahier* XII-1).

1911   *April:* Péguy publishes his *Oeuvres choisies 1900-1910* with the publisher Grasset.

June 8: The Académie française awards him the Estrade-Delcros prize (8,000 francs), instead of the Grand Prize of Literature (10,000 francs), which is not granted.

September 24: Un nouveau théologien M. Fernand Laudet shocks well-meaning Christians by celebrating "the whole of the private life, the whole of the hidden life, the whole of the non-public life" of Jesus, "who is essentially the God of the poor, of the suffering, of the workers, and therefore of those who no longer have a public life. Heaven is for the little ones" (*Cahier* XIII-2).

October 22: Written entirely in free verse, *The Portal of the Mystery of Hope* presents a meditation on the "little girl hope" (*Cahier* XIII-4).

October–December: Péguy writes the *Ballade de la peine,* the first part of the *Ballade du coeur,* a poem made up of regular quatrains in which he ruminates on his frustrated love for Blanche Raphaël (published in 1941; a complete version appears in 1975).

1912   *March 24: The Mystery of the Holy Innocents* returns to the free-verse form and deepens the meditation on childhood (*Cahier* XIII-12).

April: Writes the *Ballade de la grâce,* the second part of the *Ballade du coeur,* in which the Parable of the Prodigal Son purifies the man led astray by his passions (published in 1941; a complete version appears in 1975).

June 14–17: Makes his first pilgrimage to Chartres, accompanied by Alain-Fournier as far as Dourdan.

November 10: In the review *Le Correspondant,* Péguy publishes four *Sonnets* and *Les Sept contre Thèbes,* written in alexandrine verse.

November 25: The weekly journal *L'Opinion* publishes the poem *Châteaux de Loire.*

December 1: La Tapisserie de sainte Geneviève et de Jeanne d'Arc offers a group of poems that, beginning with a series of sonnets, culminates with a poem of nine hundred alexandrine lines on the "arms of Jesus" and the "arms of Satan" (*Cahier* XIV-5).

1913   *February 16:* *L'Argent* recalls Péguy's childhood, the young teachers, "beautiful as black hussars," who taught him about the Republic, a group of workers who loved "a work well done" (*Cahier* XIV-6): "I spent my entire childhood mending chairs with exactly the same spirit, the same heart, and the same hands, as those people built the cathedrals."

March 10: *La Grande Revue* publishes *Les Sept contre Paris*.

April 22: *L'Argent suite* praises national defense in the name of the rights of man and denounces the pacifism of Lavisse and Jaurès, while at the same time ridiculing Lanson (*Cahier* XIV-9).

May 11: Again in alexandrine verse, *La Tapisserie de Notre Dame* brings together the *Présentation de la Beauce à Notre Dame* and the *Prières dans la cathédrale de Chartres* (*Cahier* XIV-10).

July 25–28: Makes second pilgrimage to Chartres.

August: Péguy's family moves to Bourg-la-Reine, 7, rue André-Theuriet.

August 16: *La Figaro* publishes *Sainte Geneviève patronne de Paris*.

December 28: In eight thousand alexandrine lines, *Eve* presents a theological and mystical résumé of Péguy's Christianity, an epic of lost innocence and the incarnation of the Son of God in human history (*Cahier* XV-4).

1914   *January 20:* Under the pseudonym Durel, Péguy gives a commentary on *Eve* in the *Bulletin des professeurs catholiques de l'Université*, edited by Joseph Lotte.

March: The publication of *Morceaux choisis des oeuvres poétiques 1912-1913* with the publisher Ollendorff.

April 26: The *Note sur M. Bergson et la philosophie bergsonienne* makes an apology for "supple methods" as opposed to "rigid methods" (*Cahier* XV-8). "It is a supple morality, and not a rigid one, which exerts the most implacably difficult restraints. . . . That is why the most honest man is not he who follows explicit rules. Rather, it is he who stays in his place, works, suffers, and keeps silent."

May–July: Continuing the defense of Bergson, the *Note conjointe sur M. Descartes et la philosophie cartésienne* (unfinished, published in 1924) criticizes the neo-Thomists (Maritain) for having their greatest ally (Bergson) in the battle of the Gospel versus the bank-book put on the Church's Index. "We are quite right in giving bank-books to grammar school children. For we are giving them the very bible of the modern world. . . . That is to say, a license for greed and corruption in the order of the heart. . . . As the Gospels are the sum total of the whole of Christian thought, so the bank-book is the record and sum total of the whole of modern thought."

July 12: The 229th and final number of the *Cahier de la Quinzaine.*

August 2: Péguy is mobilized as a lieutenant of the reserves.

August 11–28: The Lorraine Campaign of the 19th company of the 276th infantry regiment.

August 15: Péguy attends the Mass of the Assumption in the parish of Loupmont.

August 29–September 4: The retreat on foot toward Paris.

September 5: Péguy is killed at the head of his section, near Villeroy, on the first day of the battle of la Marne.

1915   *February 4:* Charles-Pierre Péguy is born after the writer's death.

This chronology owes much to the chronologies established by Julie Sabiani (*La Ballade du coeur,* 1975), Georges Dalgues (*Cahier de l'Herne* on *Péguy,* 1977), and Simone Fraisse (*Péguy,* 1979). For the period before 1905, we have included only the principal writings of Péguy.

BIBLIOGRAPHY

For a quasi-exhaustive bibliography, refer to the *Studi su Charles Péguy, Bibliografia ed critica ed analitica (1893–1978)*, by Pia Vergine (Lecce, Milella, 1982, 2 vol., 1110 pp.). Jean Bastaire has compiled a more selective bibliography, collecting and expanding earlier ones, in the *Cahier de l'Herne* dedicated to Péguy in 1977.

Péguy's works

1. Cahiers de la Quinzaine

All of Péguy's writings published during his lifetime, except certain poems, appeared in the *Cahiers de la Quinzaine*. Available at bookstores are the series of *pré-cahiers* (1897–1899) and the first three series (1900–1902), regrouped into eleven volumes and reproduced by Slatkine reprints, distributed by Champion.

2. Complete works

Published between 1916 and 1955 with Gallimard, the collection called the *Oeuvres complètes*, comprising twenty volumes in octavo, is very useful, although it proves to be deficient in a good number of pages of prose and verse, and also in its classification of texts.

The Pléiade collection, again with Gallimard, has gradually filled these gaps. It contains three volumes: the *Oeuvres poétiques complètes* (1941, the last expanded edition in 1975), the *Oeuvres en prose 1909–1914* (1957, expanded edition in 1968), and the *Oeuvres en prose 1898–1908* (1959). A complete reissuing is in progress, under the direction of Robert Burac, which will give the whole of Péguy's writings in four volumes.

3. Standard editions

In the white collection, Gallimard has published twenty-three volumes, containing all of the essential writings in prose and in verse.

In paperback, Gallimard has published *Les Tapisseries* (1968) in the "Poetry" collection, and in the "Ideas" collection, *Notre jeunesse* (1969) and *Péguy tel qu'on l'ignore,* an anthology edited by Jean Bastaire (1975).

Two volumes edited by the *Cahiers de l'Amitié Charles Péguy,* distributed by Minard, contain the *Notes politiques et sociales,* with an introduction by André Boisserie (1957) and the *Oeuvres posthumes de Charles Péguy,* with an introduction by Jacques Viard (1969).

4. Critical editions

Only three exist:

Le Mystère de la charité de Jeanne d'Arc, with two unedited acts, a critical edition established by Albert Béguin, Club du Meilleur Livre, 1956.
La Ballade du coeur, a critical edition established by Julie Sabiani, Klincksieck, 1975.
De Jean Coste, a critical edition established by Anne Roche, Klincksieck, 1975.

5. Correspondence

The principal sources are those compiled by the *Feuillets de l'Amitié de Charles Péguy* (1948–1977) and by the bulletin *L'Amitié Charles Péguy,* which has come out regularly since 1978 (published with F. Gerbod, 35, rue du Mont-Valérien, 92210 Saint-Cloud). Here, one finds some three thousand letters written by Péguy or addressed to him.

To this we may add the following volumes:

Le Péguy que j'ai connu, by Maurice Reclus, Hachette, 1951 (letters to Geneviève Favre, the mother of Jacques Maritain).
Lettres et entretiens, presented by Marcel Péguy, Ed. de Paris, 1954 (letters to Louis Baillet and to Joseph Lotte).

Pour l'honneur de l'esprit, with an introduction and notes by Auguste Martin, Albin Michel, 1973 (letters to Romain Rolland).

Correspondance de Charles Péguy et Alain-Fournier, presentation and notes by Yves Rey-Herme, Fayard, 1973.

Claudel et Péguy, by Henri de Lubac and Jean Bastaire, Aubier, 1974.

Correspondance de Charles Péguy et Louis Boitier, presentation and commentary by Jacques Birnberg, Cahiers de l'Amitié Charles Péguy, 1976.

Correspondance de Charles Péguy et Pierre Marcel, presentation and notes by Julie Sabiani, Cahiers de l'Amitié Charles Péguy, 1980.

6. Recorded readings

Charles Péguy, texts selected by Pierre Sipriot, read by Madeleine Renaud, Claude Nollier, Alain Cuny, Pierre Vaneck, Edition Lucien Adès, 1973 (an anniversary record).

Dit Dieu, texts selected by Robert Marcy, read by Denise Bose and Robert Marcy, Edition Audivis, 1985, AV 5371 (a cassette with excerpts from the *Portal* and the *Holy Innocents*).

Studies on Péguy

There are quite a few. We will content ourselves here with pointing out the most important titles that have appeared in the last twenty-five years, with a reference to some older essays.

1. For an introduction to Péguy

Péguy, by Bernard Guyon, Hatier, in the "Connaissance des Lettres" collection, 1960; new revised edition, 1973.

Péguy, by Yves Rey-Herme, Bordas, in the "Présence littéraire" collection, 1973.

Péguy, by Simone Fraisse, Seuil, in the "Ecrivains de toujours" collection, 1979.

2. Principal studies

Saint-John Perse et quelques devanciers, études sur le poème en prose, by Monique Parent, Klincksieck, 1960 (a study on Péguy's poetical phrasing in *The Portal*).

La Gloire et la croix, vol. II: *Styles,* by Hans Urs von Balthasar, 1962, trans. R. Givord and H. Bourboulon, Aubier, 1972.

Introduction aux "Mystères" de Péguy, by Jean Onimus, Cahiers de l'Amitié de Charles Péguy, 1962.

La Religion de Péguy, by Pie Duployé, Klincksieck, 1965.

L'Univers féminin dans l'oeuvre de Péguy, by Robert Vigneault, Desclée de Brouwer, 1967.

Péguy entre Jaurès, Bergson et l'Eglise, by André Robinet, Seghers, 1968 (republished under the title *Métaphysique et politique selon Péguy*).

Péguy et Israël, by Lazare Prajs, Nizet, 1970.

Péguy et le nationalisme français, by Eric Cahm, Cahiers de l'Amitié de Charles Péguy, 1972.

Péguy soldat de la vérité, followed by *Péguy aujourd'hui,* by Roger Secrétain, Perrin, 1972.

Proust et Péguy, des affinités méconnus, by Jacques Viard, University of London, The Athlone Press, 1972.

Péguy et le monde antique, by Simone Fraisse, Colin, 1973.

Les Critiques de notre temps et Péguy, by Simone Fraisse, Garnier, 1973.

Charles Péguy, by Marie-Clotide Hubert, Bibliothèque nationale, 1974 (a catalogue of the anniversary exposition).

Claudel et Péguy, by Henri de Lubac and Jean Bastaire, Aubier, 1974.

Péguy devant Dieu, Bernard Guyon, Desclée de Brouwer, 1974.

Péguy et l'Allemagne, by Raymond Winling, université de Lille III and Champion, 1975.

Péguy et Renan, by Raymond Winling, université de Lille III and Champion, 1975.

Péguy l'insurgé, by Jean Bastaire, Payot, 1975.

Péguy et le Moyen Age, by Simone Fraisse, Champion, 1978.

Ipotesi e proposte esistenziali. Introduzione a Péguy, by Angelo Prontera, Lecce, Milella, 1980.

Ecriture et histoire dans l'oeuvre de Péguy, by Françoise Gerbod, service de reproduction des thèses, université de Lille III, 1981.

Charles Péguy, by Henri Guillemin, Seuil, 1981.

Péguy entre l'ordre et la révolution, by Géraldi Leroy, Presses de la Fondation nationale des Sciences politiques, 1981.

Péguy en son temps, by Géraldi Leroy and Julie Sabiani, Orléans, Centre Charles Péguy, 1982.

Péguy et ses "Cahiers de la Quinzaine," by Frantisek Laichter, Maison des Sciences de l'Homme et l'Amitié Charles Péguy, 1985.

3. Special issues and collections

Péguy reconnu, special issue of the review *Esprit* (August–September 1964).

Actes du colloque international d'Orléans 1964, Cahiers de l'Amitié Charles Péguy, 1966.

L'Esprit républicain, colloque d'Orléans 1970, Klincksieck, 1972.

Littérature et société, a collection presented to Bernard Guyon, Desclée de Brouwer, 1973.

Péguy, a special issue of the *Australian Journal of French Studies* 10, no. 1 (1973).

Charles Péguy et la critique littéraire de la France (March–June 1973).

Rencontres avec Péguy, colloque de Nice 1973, Desclée de Brouwer, 1975.

Péguy mis à jour, colloque de Montréal 1973, Québec, Les Presses de l'Université Laval, 1976.

Péguy, Cahier de l'Herne, 1977.

Péguy écrivain, colloque d'Orléans 1973, Klincksieck, 1978.

Péguy vivant, colloque international de Lecce 1977, Lecce, Milella, 1978.

Charles Péguy chez des protestants, special issue of the review *Foi et Vie* (March 1982).

Péguy et l'espérance, special issue of the review *Vives flammes,* Venasque, Ed. du Carmel, no. 137 (1982).

Péguy homme du dialogue, colloque en Sorbonne, 1983, Cahiers de l'Amitié Charles Péguy, 1986.

4. The "Charles Péguy" series in the Revue des Lettres Modernes

Under the direction of Simone Fraisse, the *Revue des Lettres Modernes,* edited by M.-J. Minard, published a series of issues on Péguy, each of which was dedicated to a particular theme:

Polémique et théologie, Le "Laudet" (1980).
Les "Cahiers de la Quinzaine" (1983).
Péguy romantique malgré lui (1986).

5. Older essays

Avec Charles Péguy, de la Lorraine à la Marne, by Victor Boudon, Hachette, 1916 (a revised and expanded edition was published under the title *Mon lieutenant Charles Péguy,* Albin Michel, 1964).

Notre cher Péguy, by Jérôme and Jean Tharaud, Plon, 2 vol., 1926.

Pour les fidèles de Péguy, by Jérôme and Jean Tharaud, L'Artisan du Livre, "Cahiers de la Quinzaine," new series, XVIII-12, 1927 (expanded edition, Dumas, 1949).

La Pensée de Charles Péguy, by Emmanuel Mounier, Marcel Péguy, and Georges Izard, Plon, the "roseau d'or" collection, 1931.

Péguy et les Cahiers de la Quinzaine, by Daniel Halévy, Grasset, 1941 (republished in paperback, in the "Pluriel" collection, 1979, with a preface by Robert Debré and an introduction and notes by Eric Cahm).

Le Destin de Charles Péguy, by Marcel Péguy, Perrin, 1941.

La Prière de Péguy, by Albert Béguin, Neuchâtel, Ed. de la Baconnière, "Cahiers du Rhône," Bleu III, 1942.

Jeunnesse de Péguy, by A. Mabile de Poncheville, Ed. Alsatia, 1943.

Connaissance de Péguy, by Jean Delaporte, Plon, 2 vol., 1944 (reprinted under the title *Péguy dans son temps et dans le nôtre,* coll. 10-18, 1967).

Péguy, by Romain Rolland, Albin Michel, 2 vol., 1944 (reedited with a preface by Hubert Juin and an afterword by Henri Guillemin, Edito-Service, Suisse, 1972).

Le Prophète Péguy, by André Rousseaux, Albin Michel, 2 vol., 1946.

La Poétique de Péguy, by Albert Chabanon, Robert Laffont, 1947.

L'Art de Péguy, by Bernard Guyon, Cahiers de l'Amitié Charles Péguy, 1948.

L'Eve de Péguy, by Albert Béguin, Cahiers de l'Amitié Charles Péguy, 1948 (republished with Seuil, 1955).

Les Grandes Amitié, by Raïssa Maritain, Desclée de Brouwer, 1949.

Vie et mort de Péguy, by René Johannet, Flammarion, 1950.

Le Péguy que j'ai connu, by Maurice Reclus, Hachette, 1951.
Incarnation, essai sur la pensée de Péguy, by Jean Onimus, Cahiers de l'Amitié Charles Péguy, 1952.
Péguy socialiste, by Félicien Challaye, Amiot-Dumont, 1954.
Le Vocabulaire, la syntaxe et le style des poèmes réguliers de Péguy, by Joseph Barbier, Berger-Levrault, 1957.
Péguy et le mystère de l'histoire, by Jean Onimus, Cahiers de l'Amitié Charles Péguy, 1958.
Expériences de ma vie: Péguy, by Jules Isaac, Calmann-Lévy, 1959.

6. General documentation

In 1946, an association called *L'Amitié Charles Péguy* was founded by Auguste Martin. It published a bulletin, the *Feuillets* (216 numbers, from 1948 to 1977). In 1978, the *Feuillets* were replaced by a trimestral bulletin, *L'Amitié Charles Péguy,* where one can find unedited works, testimonials, critical studies, book reviews, an annual bibliography, and any information on Péguy's influence on the world today (published with Françoise Gerbod, 35, rue du Mont-Valérien, 92210 Saint-Cloud).

The Charles Péguy Center was opened in 1960 in Orléans. As both a museum and a library, it owns nearly all of Péguy's manuscripts and the archives of the *Cahiers de la Quinzaine.* In addition to its eight thousand volumes, the Center has pictures, periodicals, and microfilm. It is open Monday through Friday (11, rue du Tabour, 45000 Orléans).

Works in English

1. Translations

Basic Verities, Prose and Poetry. Translation by Ann and Julian Green. New York: Pantheon Books Inc., 1948. An anthology of excerpts from Péguy's prose and poetry, with the translation printed alongside the original French.
God Speaks. Translation and introduction by Julian Green. New York: Pantheon Books Inc., 1945. A further selection of Péguy's poetry.
Men and Saints, Prose and Poetry. Translation by Ann and Julian Green.

New York: Pantheon Books Inc., 1944. Another anthology of excerpts, printed with the original French.

The Mystery of the Charity of Joan of Arc. Translation by Julian Green. New York: Pantheon Books Inc., 1950.

The Mystery of the Holy Innocents, and other poems. Translation by Pansy Pakenham, and with an introduction by Alexander Dru. New York: Harper, 1956.

The Portico of the Mystery of the Second Virtue. Translation by Dorothy Brown Aspinwall. Metuchen, N.J.: Scarecrow Press, 1970.

Temporal and Eternal. Translation by Alexander Dru. New York: Harper, 1958. The only translation of Péguy's prose that is not a selection of excerpts, this work contains *Notre Jeunesse* and *Clio.*

2. Books on Péguy

Adereth, M. *Commitment in Modern French Literature.* New York: Schocken Books, 1968. A study of Péguy, Aragon, and Sartre.

Dru, Alexander. *Péguy, His Prose and Poetry.* New York: Harper, 1956.

Fowlie, Wallace. *Jacob's Night, the Religious Renaissance in France.* New York: Sheed and Ward, 1947. A study on Péguy, Rouault, and Maritain.

Halévy, Daniel. *Péguy and the Cahiers de la Quinzaine.* Translation by Ruth Bethell. Denis Dobson: 1946. Halévy was a contemporary of Péguy and a financial contributor to the *Cahiers.*

Humes, Joy. *Two Against Time: A Study of the Very Present Worlds of Paul Claudel and Charles Péguy.* Distributed by the University of North Carolina Press, Chapel Hill, 1978.

Sargent, Daniel. *Four Independents.* New York: Sheed and Ward, 1935. A study on Péguy, Claudel, Hopkins, and Brownson.

Schmitt, Hans A. *Charles Péguy, the Decline of an Idealist.* Baton Rouge: Louisiana State University Press, 1967.

Servais, Yvonne. *Charles Péguy, the Pursuit of Salvation.* Westminster, Md.: Newman Press, 1953.

St. Aubyn, Frederic C. *Charles Péguy.* Boston: Twayne Publishers, 1977.

Villiers, Marjorie. *Charles Péguy: A Study in Integrity.* Westport, Conn.: Greenwood Press, 1975.

Wilson, Nelly. *Charles Péguy.* New York: Hillary House, 1965.

3. Essays and dissertations on Péguy

Balthasar, Hans Urs von. "Péguy." The concluding chapter of *The Glory of the Lord*, vol. III: *Studies in Theological Style: Lay Styles*, translated by Andrew Louth, John Saward, Martin Simon, and Rowan Williams; edited by Joseph Fessio, SJ, and John Riches. San Francisco: Ignatius Press, 1986.

Contosta, David R. *Charles Péguy, a Critic of the Modern World*. A doctoral dissertation for Miami University, 1973. An excerpt appears in *American Benedictine Review 32(2)* (June 1981).

Fanto, James. "A Conflict of Authority: The Falling Out of Lanson and Brunetière as Seen by Péguy." In *Discours et pouvoir*, edited by Ross Chambers. Ann Arbor: Department of Romance Languages, University of Michigan, 1982.

Royal, Robert. "The Literary Value of Hope: Péguy's *Porche du mystère de la deuxième vertu*." In *Play, Literature, Religion: Essays in Cultural Intertextuality*, edited and introduced by Virgil Nemoianu. Albany: State University of New York Press, 1992.

Saward, John. "The Pedagogy of Péguy." In *The Chesterton Review* 19(3) (August 1993).

Shurr, Georgia Hook. *Journey Toward Selfhood: The Role of Jeanne d'Arc in the Artistic Development of Charles Péguy*. A doctoral dissertation for the University of North Carolina at Chapel Hill, 1971.

Printed in the United States
150661LV00012B/77/P

9 780802 808998